Online Ministry Training

How Christian Leaders Institute is Equipping Called Christians for Free

Rev. Henry Reyenga

Published by Christian Leaders Institute

ISBN-10: 1479235237

ISBN-13: 978-1479235230DEDICATION

DEDICATIONS

To Rich and Helen De Vos, Ron and Cheri Parr, Richard and Barbara Gaby, Ed and Doris Van Drunen, Wayne Huizinga, Sidney Jansma Jr., Jeff Currier Sr., Milton Kuyers, Marty Ozinga III, Marty Ozinga IV, Ken and Anna Maria Adair, Case Hoogendoorn, Peter Huizenga, Brian De Cook, Steve Goudzwaard, Todd Hazelton, Paul DeBoer, Paula Heule, Grace Feddema, Marvin and Nell Feddes, Dave and Wendy Feddes and Terry Vander Aa

2 Corinthians 9:11 You will be made rich in every way so that you can be generous on every occasion, and through us your generosity will result in thanksgiving to God.

Christian Leaders Institute thanks God that each of you has a vision to develop leaders for Christ and we could serve you in your calling!

CONTENTS

PREFACE

CHRISTIAN LEADERS INSTITUTE   Tear This Form Out

Donor Information (please print) or visit
www.christianleaders.net/donate

Name _____

Address _____

City, ST Zip
Code _____

Phone: _____

Email _____

I (we) pledge a total of $_____ to be paid: ☐now
☐monthly ☐quarterly ☐yearly.

I (we) plan to make this contribution in the form of: ☐cash ☐check
☐credit card ☐other. In the USA, we will send you a receipt for your
tax deductible donation.

Credit card type |
Exp. date _____

Credit card number _____

Authorized signature _____

☐form enclosed ☐form will be forwarded

Please make checks, or other gifts | Christian Leaders Institute
payable to: | 14367 West 159th Street
                                   | Homer Glen, IL 60491

ACKNOWLEDGMENTS

I want to thank my wife, Pam, who loves and supports me.

I want to thank the leaders at Christian Leaders Institute who are passionate about leaving no one behind who is called and will do the work to be trained in ministry.

I want to thank Sonlight Curriculum. Both Dr. David Feddes's family and my family practiced years of home schooling using Sonlight Curriculum. The Sonlight curriculum was developed by John and Sarita Holzman. Home schooled parents effectively taught tens of thousands of students with Sonlight's comprehensive literature based curriculum. Sonlight showed us what was possible to be learned in the home. The methodology of CLI was influenced by Sonlight. We thank you for your inspiration.

I want to thank all of the delightful people who have supported and encouraged me since the beginning of my ministry.

I want to thank my parents, Henry and Ann Reyenga, for their support and encouragement and for living a vital walk with God.

I want to thank my brothers, John Reyenga and Richard Reyenga, for their support and encouragement.

Thanks to Debbie Darrow and my wife who helped me edit this book.

Henry Reyenga

PREFACE

I wrote this book to connect difference-makers like you to a relevant way of ministry training. I want you to see how Christian Leaders Institute utilizes cost-reducing, cutting-edge technologies that make it possible like never before to bring online ministry training to thousands.

Christian Leaders Institute (CLI) is a ministry that provides **free** online ministry training. Over twenty-two advanced ministry training classes are offered. In the 2011-2012 academic year, Christian Leaders Institute was flooded with over 14,000 new enrollments; over 1,200 are now active students.

Serve Your Mission to The World

Would you like to be part of sponsoring a student to populate the world with ministry leaders using the Internet?

CLI is giving called leaders the opportunity to earn advanced diplomas in ministry, tuition free. The aggressive use of the Internet makes this possible. Most of these called individuals would not receive excellent training without this mission.

Because the Internet makes the cost so low, our mission is to keep ministry training free of charge. We believe that Jesus did not charge his disciples, nor did Paul charge Timothy. We want to take every possible barrier away to someone getting the ministry training they need.

The Internet can bring ministry training to almost anywhere, including places like Saudi Arabia and Pakistan. We are training leaders in over 95 countries.

As you read this book, I hope that you will find this ministry to be a place for you to enthusiastically invest mission dollars. Check out www.christianleadersinstitute.org

Serve Your Calling

Are you called? Read about how Christian Leaders Institute will help you. We can give you tuition-free, high-quality ministry training. This training includes online lectures, quizzes, papers, and other interactions. As you read this book, pray about whether you are being called into ministry. Try the getting started class and see how it goes. Check out www.christianleadersinstitute.org

Serve You Locally

Does anyone from your church want to take ministry training classes? Does anyone want to meet at your church to discuss a class that several of you may take at the same time? Churches such as Covenant Life Church in Grand Haven, Michigan have sent leaders to enroll at CLI, encouraging a leader training culture. Leaders study online, get credit, and meet regularly at church to discuss what they are studying. As you read this book, you will find out if Christian Leaders Institute is right for your church.

Bring a Mission Experience to Leaders in your Church

Are you a Barnabas type? We need encouragers! Are you willing to commit a little time to chat live with students from all over the world? Many times people go on mission trips where they meet leaders and encourage them. Christian Leaders Institute seeks to bring that mission trip right into your home.

We have an "Encourager Getting Started" class that will give orientation to any of you or your church members that may be called to encourage. This encouragement is vital for international and national students who just need a little positive word or prayer. Steer encouragers to our Encourager site, which is different from our Student site, at www.christianleaders.net

This book will get you "online" to the possibilities of ministry training. You will get into the soul of Christian Leaders Institute. Find out more about Bible school, seminary-style, online ministry training at Christian Leaders Institute. I hope there is a place for you to get involved. Steve Mvondo of Cameroon got involved as a student.

"Hi, my name is Steve Mvondo, 23. I am the last born of 7 children. My mother passed 9 years ago. I live in Douala, Cameroon, Africa

I gave my life to Christ in 2001, through the testimony of one of my elder brothers, who invited me to his church. That day I was blessed by the praise, and I answered positively to the altar call. That day I really felt something different had happened in my life. I was baptized three years later.

My main ministry dream is to be a voice for God in my generation and in my country. A leader of people and a carrier of His love and grace everywhere. I want to become a pastor and a preacher.

A scholarship from Christian Leaders Institute will help me because I believe it is important to be effectively trained and well equipped for the mission. I intend to be used by God. I come from a country where it is not easy to have good training at a price I can possibly afford. A scholarship from Christian Leaders Institute will help me get closer to GOD, and to my purpose!"

Henry Reyenga

CHAPTER 1

SENDING CALLED AND TRAINED MINISTRY LEADERS

<u>1 Thessalonians 3:2</u> We sent Timothy, who is our brother and God's fellow worker in spreading the gospel of Christ, to strengthen and encourage you in your faith.

Adoniram Judson was a called leader.

Adoniram Judson was a difference-maker.

Adoniram Judson was the first American missionary at age 25, and was sent to spread Christianity in Burma in the early part of the nineteenth century. Judson had to learn the Burmese language, translate the Bible into Burmese, and translate his person into the customs of this new land. After 6 years, he welcomed his first convert into Christianity. It took 12 years for Judson to welcome 18 converts. He experienced war, imprisonment, and the deaths of his first wife, Ann, second wife, Sarah, and several children. Judson's convictions, bravery and vision have inspired thousands of missionaries who have left the land of their birth and relocated to proclaim the gospel in a new land.

Thousands of missionaries and their families have been sent. Many died en route, many died on the field proclaiming the gospel. Missionaries have been sent to large cities and remote local villages. In every populated center on earth, converts to Christianity are found and churches have been formed. Yet in every place on the earth, there are billions to be reached for Christ.

There is so much to do and opportunities to open new doors are at hand. The faithfulness of these missionaries has planted seeds for the next wave of leaders, who are being raised up and sent to do, in our time, a mission work that will change the globe.

These converts have formed a core of evangelistic capital which is ready to be identified, trained and mobilized to reach deeper into regions of the earth not yet reached.

I used to believe that we needed to set up organizations to find those who sensed the call to reach people in their own lands. This all changed in my mind when Christian Leaders Institute was founded and started offering online classes.

In 2006, we started with six students, offering seminary/Bible school training. We had no idea what would happen. For the first few years we were figuring out how to effectively utilize the technology. But by 2012, over fourteen thousand new students had enrolled and over twelve hundred students are actually receiving advanced training.

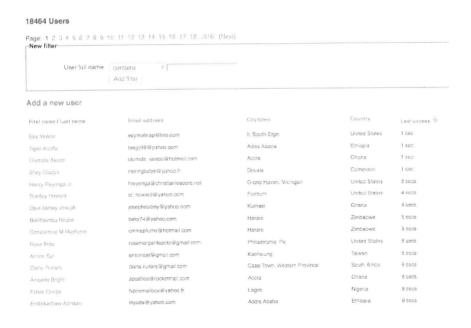

God has compelled "called" believers from every place on earth to seek advanced ministry training in English using the Internet at Christian Leaders Institute (CLI). This is only the beginning.

For the first time in history, technological tools exist to deliver advanced academic ministry training to leaders anywhere in the world.

The missionary leadership capital is in place whereby Christian mentors and pastors are able to provide a local context for students that enroll at CLI.

Christian Leaders Institute is committed to encouraging the called to go as far as they can go in getting the training they need to effectively lead in their local community. We believe the currency of ownership in ministry training will be "calling" and not money.

Christian Leaders Institute seeks to identify called leaders who have the gifts, competencies, temperament and passion to reach people.

Christian Leaders Institute encourages those who possess the Biblical qualifications of being an office bearer, as found in 1 Timothy 3, as those who are actually called into ministry.

Christian Leaders Institute believes that this new wave of called leaders are largely going to be bi-vocational and that they will not necessarily be called with the expectation of becoming full-time paid clergy.

Christian Leaders Institute is very aware of reproducible systems and structures that last way beyond our time. A student of CLI will be taught how to have a simple, reproducible walk with God in their personal life, with their family, and supported by their church. This walk is to be shared with those who do not have a walk with God. The "Getting Started" class introduces a reproducible walk as the foundation for being a Christian leader.

Christian Leaders Institute believes that we have the opportunity to bring formerly very expensive Biblical academic training to every place the Internet is connected. This training is not just content that is put up on a website; this is training and an interactive connection, including quizzes and input from a knowledgeable staff of leaders.

Christian Leaders Institute believes that this technology represents an opportunity for supporting, encouraging and becoming involved in a great open door to ministry training.

Investing in Currency of Calling

When Judson arrived in Burma in 1820, there was no Christian culture, no churches, no pastors. There was no Christian "capital." Judson and his wife, Ann, were the only Christians in the nation. There was no Christian leadership capital or assets that could be accessed in the country. Judson's calling to evangelize the world was the "currency" he brought to Burma. This ministry currency has always been used by God to build the kingdom of God. Jesus called the twelve disciples. Ordinary men whose calling would change the world. Paul and Barnabas were called, and with that currency the early church began building ministry capital in the Roman empire.

Today in Myanmar, formerly Burma, there are churches and leaders who reach the lost and disciple those in their congregations. The investments made one hundred and ninety-two years ago by Judson are now bringing in dividends. All over the world there is missionary capital that can be built on to increase its effectiveness. At Christian Leaders Institute we meet potentially-called church leaders every fifteen minutes. They trace their spiritual family tree to the missions movements. In most areas of the world this capital exists.

Our goal at Christian Leaders Institute is to invest more into building on the ministry capital that already exists within the local church. We position our training to support the pastors, leaders and mentors of individual churches, and they rise up as leaders to reach people in their local areas. The academic ministry content is effectively delivered to students who stay with their local leaders. This is the type of investment that enhances and builds more Christian culture. Our currency is calling. If a leader is called to serve Christ, we want to make sure that currency is placed into the service of building the kingdom of God.

Who Are The Called Who Attend Christian Leaders Institute?

As you consider attending, encouraging students or investing mission dollars into Christian Leaders Institute, you may want to know who attends right now.

Christian Leaders Institute includes students from every continent, representing over 95 countries. The nations with the largest representation include the USA, Ghana, Nigeria, Canada, Uganda, the Philippines, Pakistan, India, South Africa and Kenya. Christian Leaders Institute is also becoming large in the islands of the world.

Characteristics of Christian Leaders Institute students:

1. Indigenous and Committed to be that way:

    Christian Leaders Institute students are generally very committed to staying in their countries. They sign up because they have access to high-quality ministry training in their local context. They have not been asking if CLI training will help them move to another country. They want to stay and minister where they are placed by the Lord. Take Fikre Fikadu of Ethiopia, for example.

"I live in Ethiopia. I was born in a partially Christian family. And I grew up in church hearing the word of God through Sunday school. When I had been reached at seventeen; my walk with God was completely corrupted by the peer pressure and I was lost in the worst addictions; like hard drinking, cigarettes, gambling and all bad experiences.

At that time many pastors and my Christian youth friends were trying hard to reach me back to the Lord, but I first rejected them. I was sinking into the deep of worldly things and I have connected all my styles with the technological developments now available here.

However, I am always marveling at in my life, even in my worst conditions, God would never let me down!

Radical changes occurred in my life after my Lord God visited me with his merciful eyes. I received grace before him and all men. Today even if there are some challenges in my life; my joy is now in the Lord!

My major ministry dream is to reach the lost and those who are under the devil's captivity bringing them to the Lord.

God is good! I hope that as God raised Christian Leaders Institute for the benefit of many servants of the Gospel like me.

To tell you the truth at this time I could not afford payment for learning. So, CLI is very important for the realization of my childhood dreams by having the chance of acquiring a good knowledge about the Lord and scripture with the help of the Holy Spirit."

2. Generally Poor in Monetary Resources

Christian Leaders Institute students are poor, but have enough resources and social capital to have received an education and to have access to the Internet. We will even receive phone calls from cell phones in Africa concerning a question. We habitually invite students to donate to Christian Leaders Institute, and though they do not have large amounts to give, they still give generously. We have received $200-$300 contributions from students in Africa, for instance.

In America, the demographic includes: urban and rural poor who have little else than an Internet connection, disabled leaders, leaders in the Christian Reformed or Reformed Church who know some of the instructors, home-schooled graduates, and a large group of fifty-year-old and above leaders who are sensing a calling into ministry later in life.

3. Bi-vocational Leaders

We have noticed that CLI is supporting those leaders who really want to explore a bi-vocational vision. CLI students generally expect they will be working bi-vocationally in their country of residence. While the allure of an invitation to study in western countries will entice some of the brightest and most academically wired students into western programs, our students will be passed over for these expensive programs and ordinarily will stay in their own country to become pastors, whether they receive quality ministry training or not.

They are hard working Christians who are called to bi-vocational ministry. Many times these leaders are called to become pastors and teachers. Some times these leaders are called to start ministries.

Take, for example, Tony Wetmore of Crestline, California, USA. He is taking the Christian Leaders Training so that he can more effectively start a ministry. Listen to his story.

"My name is Tony, and I live in a small town called Crestline, in California, USA. Within an hour drive is the Los Angeles basin, where millions and millions of people live, most in darkness, many in addiction, in jail, on the streets, and lost, hurting, without hope. I believe my country has become mostly post Christian. I believe it's time to shred the darkness, and turn up the LIGHT!

I'm a believer and follower of Jesus Christ. I came to the Lord at YMCA camp when I was 12, and participated in youth groups through high school. I fell away from the Lord shortly after graduating, and spent 10 years in the "world." I then reconnected with the Lord, and became born again. I'm married to a wonderful wife for 25+ years, and have 3 incredible children. I have always been a ministry leader in my church - Youth, Homeless, Prison, and Worship Leader to name a few. I am a First Responder/Emergency Medical Technician on a 911 ambulance in Riverside County, where I am able to pray over, and with, my patients in times of crisis and need.

My ministry dreams are to become a non-profit 501(c) 3, and create a ministry, Church, and program that serve all of "the least of these." Matthew 25:31-40. To tell people, lost people, hurting people, abused people, and young people about the love and saving grace that can only come through our Lord and Savior, Jesus Christ. To help make the change from bread and water of this world, to the bread of life, and living water of Jesus Christ!

A scholarship with CLI will work around my very difficult work schedule, and ministry life, and will give me the much needed ability and knowledge to minister and pastor better, more completely, and more intelligently, to this hurting world."

4. Technologically Savvy

We have noticed that our students are technologically savvy even if they live in the remotest parts of the world. Internet access is more common than sewer lines in some countries.

In places like America, the United Kingdom, South Africa, and other western nations, the students who apply, though poorer by the standards of their mainline culture, navigate the web very well and ordinarily know exactly what to do to succeed at CLI. We noticed that many retired called ministry leaders will actually get their children to explain how to interact better through the technology of the Internet.

When we started offering online classes in 2006, many remote places of the world were not ready for online training. Today, I am at times surprised at how savvy students really are as they upload files, and do YouTube videos for the preaching class. I believe that we have only just begun to see how effectively new Christian leaders can be trained online!

5. Ordained Pastors lacking respected Ministry
Training

There is a large group of CLI applicants that
already have been ordained as pastors or church
planters. Sadly, many of them have been
desperately seeking advanced training. In many
places in the world, targeted missions money
supporting specific mission goals has supplied only
certain training, neglecting to meet other
important needs of pastors and church leaders.

This is especially true with church planting
training. Large western ministries have invested in
helping bi-vocational leaders to plant a church.
But these same leaders are not given training in

other areas that western pastors are trained in at seminary. This causes sustainability issues. It is difficult for the development of a full sphere of Christian culture to be cultivated by these leaders.

These leaders have expressed great disappointment over this situation. They communicate that they feel like second-class pastors because the pastors that do receive the western-supported training are considered more qualified and are given more opportunities, not based on the quality of their walk, their ministry effectiveness, or the specifics of their calling and gifts, but simply on their connection to the western-prescribed training path.

The training opportunities that are funded for these leaders are dumbed down or specialized in such a way that it leaves most indigenous pastors lacking the standing they need to really thrive in their country.

Christian Leaders Institute is committed to giving a ministry training that allows graduates the standing to thrive even in relationship to pastors that have attended traditional residential seminaries.

6. Educated

Christian Leaders Institute students are smart. They know how to communicate. They are often bi-lingual, with English being their second language. Large percentages of them would thrive at residential seminaries, but would never have the opportunity to enroll, because they were too poor or their situation in life prohibited residential ministry training.

7. Respected in Their Culture

In countries that are not hostile to Christianity, our students are highly respected. Even clergy in their country who had residential training from western sources are mentoring students from CLI and encouraging them to get their diplomas.

8. Generally Older and Already Tested

We have noticed that four out of five of our students are 35 and older. These older students are not in a position to go to a residential program. Distance-learning programs are also difficult and still too expensive. This group of leaders is generally not going to move anywhere.

9. Often in Countries where it is difficult to lead in Christianity

We have noticed that CLI can offer training to places that Christianity is having difficulty penetrating. We have trained students in Pakistan, Saudi Arabia, and Libya to name a few. Our students get the training to create Christian culture, despite the resistance of their country. Sadly, we suspect that some of our students have been persecuted for their Christian witness. We do everything we can to keep their identities secret.

10. Very Remote Places

We are training students in remote islands where western missions money would never be able to support quality ministry training. These students are being trained in places like Samoa, Martinique and St. Kitts.

11. Disabled Students

We are training students who have been disabled and are called. Christian Leaders Institute has taken the training to their homes where they can access this training, fitting their specific challenges. I have been moved to praise God when I hear some of the stories of those who face such challenges.

What about digital chaplains? Chaplains who can "chat" with people who need ministry? Christian Leaders Institute bought the domain names, "chatplain.com -.org. Notice the spelling, "chatplain" similar to "chaplain." I would love to start a ministry where we mobilize Christian leaders to "chat" and minister to people in need interacting on the Internet. It is exciting to consider all the different ways that God can use his people to minister to others.

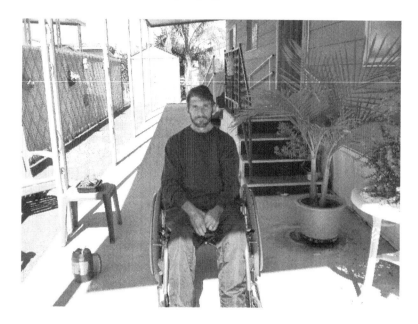

Mark writes,

"Hello, my name is Mark Ziegelhoefer. I'm 53yrs old and blessed to be born into an Orthodox Jewish family. Temporarily, I'm paraplegic due to a spinal injury, which is drug-related, consequences of my past sins. Also, I have been diagnosed with Hepatitis C, drug-related as well.

Now, I am awaiting the Lord's perfect timing for my physical healing. In August 2001, the Lord brought me a beautiful woman, who is now my wife, Kerrie. She has been a Christian since her childhood. In 2004, I accepted Jesus Christ as my Lord and Savior. Since I have past experience of 32yrs in drug abuse, my dream is to help others that are still struggling with chemical addictions. Knowing Jesus was the only way that I was able to overcome drugs, I want to help lead others to Jesus. I tried all the other ways to freedom from drugs and I know for a fact that Jesus is the only way."

12. Immigrants

Many students have immigrated to new countries looking for new opportunities. Countries like Great Britain, Spain and Canada. These students come with fresh enthusiasm combining love for their new country with a passion to share Christ. Take Rosette Singson, she immigrated to Canada.

"I live in Alberta, Canada - our Promised Land. For the past few years that I've been here, I noticed that every single moment of the day, lots and lots of people need Christ in order to cope with life's challenges. Because of the lies and darkness that the enemy is inflicting to every human being, I felt the desire to do something for Christ's Kingdom.

It is in the midst of my troubles, my pain and suffering that I encountered Christ. So, I thought, it is just right to share Him to others whose only hope is Christ. It is my dream to see the lost restored and find the Way, The Truth and The Life - Jesus - through my ministry.

I continue to believe for God's guidance and intervention towards the ministry and the calling He has for me. He is the Alpha and the Omega."

13. Very willing to contribute

Many students are doing what they can to donate back to Christian Leaders Institute. We are praying that as our students graduate and plant and pastor churches, they will be able to contribute more and become mentors for future students, making better and better training available to church leaders.

Is this "Free" Opportunity a Good Idea?

Christian Leaders Institute offers free tuition. Why? Many have asked this. Some have wondered whether it will be valued if it is free. Some have said that we have so many students, let them pay for it themselves. Others have said that you will never be a sustainable ministry unless the students pay and outside funding is not needed.

I have reflected on this a long time. I have prayed about this much. I have researched business models and consulted with traditional institutions.

I read the Bible and do not see a charge for training people to be leaders. I just can't see that Peter and John gave tuition to Jesus in the form of currency. The only currency that was given was the currency of calling. "Come follow me." That was it! When they followed

Jesus, He trained them to be the first leaders in the new church. Jesus had his supporters who paid for the training culture. First there was God, the Father and the power of the God-head. When they needed to pay taxes, they had the option of getting currency out of a fish. I love how Jesus funded a tax they had to pay, "But so that we may not offend them, go to the lake and throw out your line. Take the first fish you catch; open its mouth and you will find a four-drachma coin. Take it and give it to them for my tax and yours." (Matthew 17:27).

Jesus also had financial supporters such as Joseph of Arimathea. We don't know whether he contributed to Jesus while Jesus was training his disciples, but we do know that his funding of Jesus's ministry at his death illustrated the faithful involvement of a truly "board level" supporter.

"Now there was a man named Joseph, a member of the Council, a good and upright man, who had not consented to their decision and action. He came from the Judean town of Arimathea and he was waiting for the kingdom of God. Going to Pilate, he asked for Jesus' body. Then he took it down, wrapped it in linen cloth and placed it in a tomb cut in the rock, one in which no one had yet been laid." (Luke 23:50-53).

After Pentecost, we see the out-pouring of support for the early church by people like Barnabas. "Joseph, a

Levite from Cyprus, whom the apostles called Barnabas (which means Son of Encouragement), sold a field he owned and brought the money and put it at the apostles' feet." (Acts 4:36-37). Barnabas was an ideal "board level" supporter and sponsor. He not only contributed to the funding of the church, he also helped expand the number of leaders by sponsoring Paul and connecting him to the apostles. Barnabas had credibility with the apostles. He was an encourager, supporter and networker for the development of leadership capital.

It appears that Barnabas offered his mentorship of Paul free of charge. Paul did have to support himself as a tentmaker while he was being trained and made ready. Barnabas was so committed to ministry training that it even created a disagreement between himself and Paul. Barnabas, being Barnabas, wanted to give a younger leader, Mark, a second opportunity. Paul did not want to drag the missions march down with someone that may not work out. Barnabas and Paul separated. Later Mark and Paul worked closely together. Mark hung out with Peter, who helped him write the gospel of Mark.

Paul went on to do ministry training with lots of leaders like Titus and Timothy. Most of these early leader recruits were bi-vocational and we have good reason to believe that their ministry training was free.

I believe that there are leaders like Joseph of Arimathea and Barnabas who provide the leadership capital for the development of Christian leaders.

No One Missed

Christian Leaders Institute desires to make ministry training tuition-free so no viable, called leaders are missed. I believe that the time is short until Jesus comes and we have so much to do. This mission is mobilizing a large number of trained ministry leaders. As you read this book, you get more of an idea of why it is possible to be ambitiously training thousands of church leaders. The leaders are out there waiting to be trained.

"It was He who gave some to be apostles, some to be prophets, some to be evangelists, and some to be pastors and teachers, to prepare God's people for works of service, so that the body of Christ may be built up." (Ephesians 4: 11-12).

The Profile of the Intrinsically Motivated

Finally, free tuition is a test. Those that do well with free tuition are motivated internally at a deeper level. Charging tuition does bring a form of ownership, to the point that the ministry training is given a monetary value which helps in creating a force to complete the studies.

When something labor intensive like ministry training is free, the prime force the student has is his God-motivated call into the ministry. Students loose nothing if they stop their training. They gain greatly if they finish their training.

The profiles of the students that complete classes at Christian Leaders Institute are profiles of "called" leaders who completes goals and challenges because they need to and want to!

CHAPTER 2

TAKE THE DISTANCE OUT OF DISTANCE LEARNING

<u>1 Corinthians 9:22-23</u> To the weak I became weak, to win the weak. I have become all things to all men so that by all possible means I might save some. I do all this for the sake of the gospel, that I may share in its blessings.

What would happen if Joshua invented an energy conversion box? This box could convert air into electricity. The invention is scalable. Little boxes replace batteries, which power computers and other such devices. Small boxes energize cars, small generators and wells in remote areas. Big convertor boxes could run industrial applications and power plants. The design is simple and maintenance costs are very low. Joshua's concept is simple to the point that it could be copied easily and would supply a productive resource that would enhance the lives of billions of people.

New wells could be dug and a conversion box generator would run a little motor that pumped fresh water to those who needed it. Cars would no longer need gas and carbon pollution could be seriously reduced. Trains never need to burn stinky diesel fuel, and goods and services could be brought to the market for a fraction of the cost. Propeller airplanes would make a comeback and these planes would never run out of fuel. The effects of this discovery would change the world quickly.

But wait! Not everyone would be excited about this new technology. Those in the energy field would be negatively affected. In a period of thirty years, most fossil fuel companies would be unneeded. Other industries would also be affected. Nuclear power plants would be able to be replaced with motors, which would generate electricity all powered by "air."

Some people would not be excited about this technology for other reasons. They would not care about carbon emissions and would never consider getting an "electric" car. For them, the sound of the gas engine and the noise is what makes a car a car.

Many unions would rise up to stop this conversion box. Imagine the jobs lost.

Governments would want to control this technology quickly. Imagine war equipment running on a cheap power supply.

Imagine that Joshua decided he would give this technology away before anyone tried to own it and make money on it. He legally made it public domain and sent all the secrets for its development and design to everyone. He did not benefit financially from it, nor did he care about financial reward. It was his gift to humanity, period.

Over a period of time, every industry, government, and people group would somehow incorporate this invention. Some companies would keep their old technology and use only small contributions of the convertor box design; other companies would redesign their entire product lines around this resource. Some companies would go out of business and new companies would form. The world would be a different place.

The Internet is like the "Conversion Box"

The Internet has changed the world radically when it comes to the exchange of information and resources. While the invention of the computer was revolutionary, the Internet has brought a new form of connectivity that has changed how everything from relationships to exchange of information works. Many authors and commentators have chronicled the massive changes that have taken place.

Type into the Google search box, "How the Internet has changed the world," to get thousands of hits from news articles to academic papers. Many saw the significance of the Internet, but many did not see it as a threat to how they operated. The changes that have and will occur because of the Internet are so many and varied that almost no one argues that they can even be overstated.

For instance, the Internet has changed our behaviors and practices in many ways. Here are a few examples:

- How someone buys almost anything, including airline tickets, travel arrangements, books and e-books, golf clubs and poodles.

- How someone communicates with other people. First there was e-mail. Now social networking sites such as Facebook and Google Plus have connected over ½ billion people. These social networking sites are replacing phone directories. Someone is more likely to connect via Facebook then actually make a physical phone call.

- How someone researches information. Google, Yahoo and Bing are really just digital libraries. While there is misinformation on the Internet, a discerning researcher would rather have a library brought into their own home or workplace to research anything from where to eat to what poodle to buy using the Internet.

- How politicians are elected. Blogs and Vlogs, social media, and other ways of using the Internet are now often a factor between who gets elected.

- How likeminded people find each other. Likeminded researchers can now connect instantly from different places of the world to compare notes as they solve problems together. Those interested in eating organic foods can chat, blog, message and build organic food culture together.

- How knowledge and teachings are transmitted to individuals. The development of Wikipedia and TEDs University has become a resource that many use as they seek knowledge and training about a whole host of topics. Some schools and universities have jumped on the bandwagon, offering distance-learning classes that allow students to do classes online and get credit at the academic institution.

The Impact on Ministry Training

Increasingly, the Internet will have a bigger role in equipping called leaders for ministry. The Internet cannot be ignored. It has changed the way humans learn. It has changed the way information is transmitted. It has provided a tool for interaction that can be used effectively in providing accountability and interaction. Open-source programs like Moodle.org allow schools and institutions to interact in a world-class way with students.

Christian Leaders Institute has a meaningful interactive relationship with thousands of ministry students.

Student Profiles

When students are accepted, they receive a student profile which places them on our roster. After they are fully accepted they enroll in classes they need for their certificate of diploma goals. The students are given a special enrollment key that places them on class rosters.

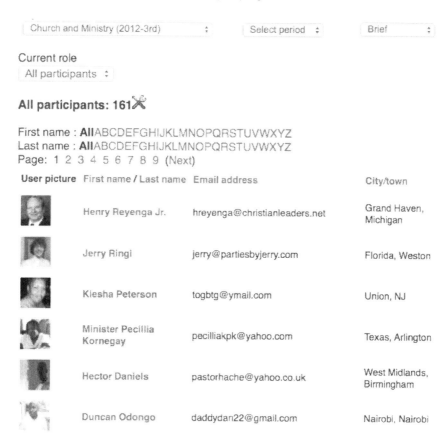

Online Lectures

The professors prepare and place lectures in the digital syllabus. This lecture can be viewed over and over again. Every time students view lectures, those viewings are recorded in student viewing logs. In other words, the professors know which students are watching the lectures.

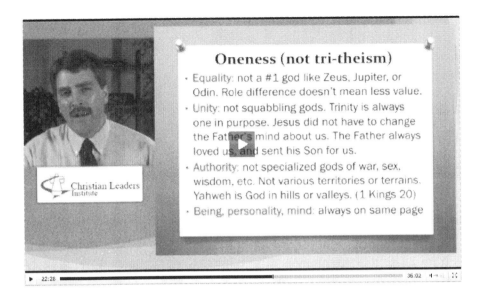

Quizzes and Examinations

Christian Leaders Institute professors assign students quizzes and examinations of their learning. The quiz and examination grades are automatically recorded and saved. At the end of the semester, the quiz results are automatically tallied and a grade for each class is assigned. There are technological safeguards that make it very hard for students to cheat. While this all sounds complicated, the fact is that the quizzes and examinations and the professors involvement with the students work is presented to both students and professors with an easy interface.

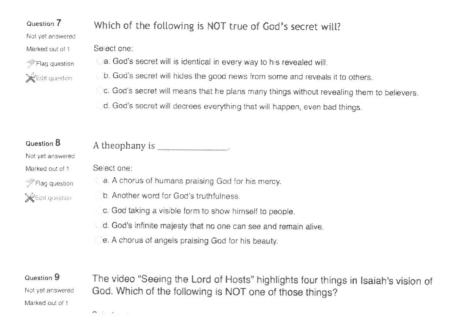

Question 7

Not yet answered

Marked out of 1

Flag question

Edit question

Which of the following is NOT true of God's secret will?

Select one:

a. God's secret will is identical in every way to his revealed will.

b. God's secret will hides the good news from some and reveals it to others.

c. God's secret will means that he plans many things without revealing them to believers.

d. God's secret will decrees everything that will happen, even bad things.

Question 8

Not yet answered

Marked out of 1

Flag question

Edit question

A theophany is _____.

Select one:

a. A chorus of humans praising God for his mercy.

b. Another word for God's truthfulness.

c. God taking a visible form to show himself to people.

d. God's infinite majesty that no one can see and remain alive.

e. A chorus of angels praising God for his beauty.

Question 9

Not yet answered

Marked out of 1

The video "Seeing the Lord of Hosts" highlights four things in Isaiah's vision of God. Which of the following is NOT one of those things?

Students Submit Papers

Students watch lectures, take quizzes and tests, but also participate in submitting papers and even submitting YouTube student produced sermons for evaluation. There are so many features that I could tell you about, but I do not want to make this book into a technology manual for internet ministry training.

The technology is so effective and inexpensive that Christian Leaders Institute can offer an online ministry training education for a fraction of what traditional seminaries can offer. It is so efficient that Christian Leaders Institute can make high impact with a smaller budget than traditional ministry training organizations.

The Internet allows Christian Leaders Institute to return to practices that are very ancient in the identifying and training of a Christian leader ready for ministry. To get a fuller understanding of why something so cutting edge as the Internet can help us return to something so ancient, let's look at the ancient practices of ministry training.

Ancient Biblical Practices of Ministry Training

In the Old Testament, prophets were trained at the school of the prophets. A snap shot into this culture is easily seen with the life, ministry and work of Elijah and Elisha. In those days, three thousand years ago, there were seminaries for various religions. There were schools for Baal worship where Baal leaders were raised up to promote the Baal religion. In Israel in 1000 BC, the king and queen of Israel, Ahab and Jezebel, were big supporters of the Baal religion. In fact, they were making the national religion of Israel to be the worshiping of Jezebel's god, the god of Ekron.

The minority religion was the religion of Yahweh. Elijah was the only prophet left with 7000 people that did not worship Baal. Elijah began a school of the prophets by calling Elisha and calling him into the service of the Lord. By the time of Elijah's death, Elisha was ready to take the mantle. Elisha expanded this school even more.

How were the prophets trained? Basically, they just spent time being mentored by their leaders until they were ready to be prophets themselves. This was clearly a mentor model, where local mentorship raised up prophets. The leading prophet modeled to and taught the called, yet-to-be trained, new prophet the way of the Lord.

In the New Testament, Jesus sets up a school of the prophets, whom he calls disciples. The Son of God calls ordinary people, usually from the working class, fishermen and tax collectors, to be future prophets or disciples. We see in his ministry that Jesus knows the Old Testament and spends his time sharing and teaching insights about the kingdom of God that would be ushered in when Jesus himself would die, rise from the dead, and ascend on high.

Jesus also promoted the mentor model, where a long-term relationship accompanies teaching, which prepared the disciples to be the prophets of the early church. Especially interesting is how the leaders of the Jewish religion characterized Peter and John after Jesus had ascended to be with God. The Jewish leaders noted, "When they saw the courage of Peter and John and realized that they were unschooled, ordinary men, they were astonished and they took note that these men had been with Jesus." (Acts 4:13).

The mentor model was the model that drove ministry training in the Old and New Testament. When the apostle Paul was chosen as God's instrument to spread the church to the Gentiles, he too worked with a mentor model, which included spending time with the newly-called future prophets. A great example of this is his work with Timothy, who he called his son. First and Second Timothy are examples of mentor "content" that even forms part of Scripture.

By the time the apostles had passed away, their teachings and the teachings of Christ were written down for the Christian leaders to pass on the knowledge content of the faith to newly-called prophets. The mentorship model was firmly the dominant model for the identifying, training and mobilizing of future prophets, or, as they were then called, pastors. Pastor training was clearly a mentoring operation that included communicating the content of the faith.

This discipleship model yielded elders, deacons and pastors who populated the leader teams of the early church. They were used by God to spread the gospel, and the church spread quickly. This mentor model gradually changed to a more corporate model for the training of leaders.

Within five hundred years, the church organization developed and resembled the cultural organizations of the time. The monastic movement developed where leaders were cloistered away from the very culture they were called to reach. Even though these developments themselves did not stop the church from proclaiming Christ as Lord, a drift occurred and the church soon was focused on perpetuating its organization as much as a walk with God in Christ.

The Development of Traditional Seminaries

By the time of the Reformation, very little scripture was actually used to instruct the prophets. Instead, church traditions and practices, as they developed, formed the core curriculum that was communicated to leaders of the church.

At that time, God raised up reformers and the technology of the printing press, allowing the original words that taught Timothy to now be the core curriculum for future church leaders. The printing press changed everything. Once the actual words of the Old and New Testament formed the content of the faith that was to be passed down, a major reformation occurred.

This scriptural content was new again on the scene. Catechisms like the Westminster Confession and the Heidelberg Catechism were brought to the center as confessions that elevated scripture as the only rule for life and teaching. The early monastic (seminary) model was continued from the Catholic Church, but the content was now influenced from Scriptures and the confessions of faith.

The word seminary is from the Latin, "seminarium", which means seed-bed. Catholics started calling their ministry training institutions "seminaries" at the time of the counter-reformation. At these seminaries they stressed personal discipline and philosophy. The "seed," though, for seminary training, was to take someone out of their context and place them in an institutional setting for training and education.

Comparisons of Ministry Training Models

If we compare the seminary model with the discipleship model, we have to be very careful not to talk about the advantages of one model while criticizing the disadvantages of the other model. We have seen much blessing and challenge from both models of ministry training. Let's compare them.

The Discipleship Model Strengths:

> Local and contextual: New pastors and church planters are mentored locally, and this local connection makes them more effective as they minister to the specific people group they are involved with.

Personal Endorsements: The mentoring leaders are usually familiar with the discipleship struggles their mentees encounter.

Cost-Effective: The ministry overhead of classrooms and professors is not needed.

Ministry Opportunities: Effective mentoring pastors provide opportunities for ministry involvement.

New pastors do not have to relocate or incur great expenses; the acceptance of the calling is the focus. This is friendlier to the families of the called leaders.

More leaders can be cultivated for the service of Christ.

This model is more conducive for the development of bi-vocational leaders. Leaders do not accumulate debt and do not need higher salaries to support their serving in ministry.

The Discipleship Model Weaknesses:

Varied Mentors: Many pastors are not that skilled at transferring knowledge and insights for ministry training.

Local Situation Dramas: Sometimes those who are called into ministry threaten the ministry pastors or mentors.

Accreditation: If someone wants to get an advanced degree, this model does not conform to that desire.

Denominations often do not have a good referral system for this model and many times consider their ministry candidates to be less qualified because of their perceived lack of academic training.

The Traditional Seminary Model Strengths:

Accreditation: Many seminaries offer accreditation that allows students to move on toward advanced degrees.

Connections: Many seminaries have connections in denominations that allow them to move around to existing churches and even receive funding for the planting of new churches. Many times these seminaries have connections for ordination within the denomination.

Objective Tests: When leaders leave their local context they are tested personally and this test often forces them to trust God more.

Accountable Academic Training: The paid staff of seminaries specifically holds their students to academic standards that assure academic competency.

The Traditional Seminary Model Weaknesses:

Eliminates Some Called Leaders: Seminaries tend to focus on academics to the point that many called leaders will not succeed at these accredited institutions.

Costly: Most seminary tracks for ministry training are very costly from many perspectives. Tuition, moving, books and many more expenses put people's lives on hold for four or five years.

Not Bi-vocationally Friendly: Seminaries tend to not serve the needs of leaders who are called later in life and seek to keep their daily work.

Christian Leaders Institute Approach

The tools of the Internet offer, for some, exciting options that connect the strengths of both models and minimize some weaknesses. There will never be a completely perfect model for ministry training, but Christian Leaders Institute will try to make it possible for every called leader to do well in ministry.

Born Out of Walls Hits

When Christian Leaders Institute was formed, we wanted to mobilize called leaders into ministry. We began by using the discipleship model. We had discovered this model with others in the last decade of the 20th century. We were working this model for many years and hit the walls of the weaknesses of this type of training while continuing to enjoy the strengths of the discipleship model.

At around 2003, it become apparent to me, at Christian Leaders Institute, that some of the weaknesses of the discipleship model needed to be addressed so as to equip more sustainable leaders. Many times I encountered leaders who were so excited about their calling. Many wanted to serve as bi-vocational leaders. But many struggled because they did not have the knowledge and insights needed for long-term confidence and sustainability in the ministry.

I was praying and looking for a way to bring accessible opportunity for training to called leaders. At the same time, advancements in Internet technology were making it possible to put classes on the Internet that could be accessed efficiently and inexpensively.

I started taking technology classes at the local community college. Through the generous donations of a few leaders and foundations, I hired a technology specialist from the University of Chicago, named Jerry Lorenz. Christian Leaders Institute offered online classes in 2006 with six students signed up for training. Most of the classes were just guided self-study, but we found them to be effective in training bi-vocational leaders.

In 2008, I invited Dr. David Feddes to join CLI as the first provost. Dr. Feddes had served as the English radio minister for the Back to God Hour for 14 years and had just completed his Doctorate in Cultural studies from Trinity University in Deerfield, IL. Dr. Feddes had also worked with me in planting a bi-vocational church in Monee, IL.

In 2012, I became full-time in leading Christian Leaders Institute to effectively reproduce leaders.

The Christian Leaders Institute Approach

Christian Leaders Institute seeks to combine the benefits of both the discipleship model and the seminary model for ministry training. The goal is to mobilize as many effective and sustainable Christian leaders as possible for ministry. The revolutionary impact of the Internet allows us to venture into seeking to bring the best of both approaches.

The ministry training approach of Christian Leaders Institute seeks to do the following:

1. Respect Local Mentors/Sponsors

Charlie Post was 67 years old when called into the ministry. He was encouraged to enroll at CLI by his pastor, Rev. Tom Groelsema, in Byron Center, MI. Charlie was considered too old by many to receive a call, but Tom encouraged him to take that next step. Tom would meet with Charlie along the way to encourage him and share pastoral insights. Charlie got his ministry diploma and he's now preaching at churches, nursing homes and the gospel mission. Tom organized a time where Charlie received his diploma in front of the Elders and Deacons of his church.

Local pastors and church leaders see the doctrine and life of their members close up. These local leaders have made a commitment to bring those in their charge to their next step in ministry preparation, whether that is just teaching a class or, like in the case of Charlie Post, encouraging him to receive advanced ministry training.

Christian Leaders Institute is designed to encourage local mentors to help local leaders take that next step. On the application of new students, we ask them to designate a mentor and a local pastor. This lets the student know that they are connected. We find that almost everyone has a local leader who they are connected to in their ministry journey. CLI considers those local mentors as "adjunct faculty".

If students do not have a local mentor or pastor who mentors them, we find that those students usually drop out. Christian Leaders Institute includes assignments where the student brings work completed to the local mentor or pastor to discuss. This relationship is very valuable and we find it very important in the preparing of a church leader.

2. Accessible and Mission Driven

Because the ministry cost in comparison to traditional ministry training schools is so low, we make this available to any called leaders, offering the training tuition free of charge. Ultimately, it may be free to the student, but it is not easy. Humans have the currency of time or money. We take the money equation out of the mix. Since the Internet platform is so efficient, we are able to make this truly a mission that foundations, individuals, and students can support with a great return for their ministry investment. The funding model of CLI leverages kingdom resources to make high-quality ministry training free of charge.

Some have objected to the "free" part because they feel that people will not value what they do not pay for. The fact is that if someone will not value their ministry training unless they have to pay for it, maybe they should find a place to purchase that training. CLI wants intrinsically called pastors who will value their training simply because they need it. We also find that those leaders, when asked to donate for the training of others, are so willing to help.

The other issue is that if Christian Leaders Institute opened up a tuition department, it would add to overhead, and that cost would prevent CLI from reaching even more leaders to train.

The challenge for Christian Leaders Institute is to find more donors who see this as a great opportunity to invest in the future leaders of the Church worldwide. We will also seek to be supported by the churches that our graduates pastor and lead.

3. Appropriate Academic Expectations

When the Discipleship model re-asserted itself in the 1990s, there was great optimism that this was going to unleash a new age of ministry preparation. The fact was that many were recruited to be pastors, received some training, often in specialized areas like church planting, but these leaders did not get enough of the academic training they needed. Many failed.

The Bible, church, people and their souls, contemporary society, different questions about God and faith, pastoral care, church leadership, and so much more are all areas that pastors have to be competent and knowledgeable about. It is unwise to just give new called leaders barely enough and hope that they will sink or swim in ministry.

This attitude of giving them just enough has made many lessen their confidence in the discipleship model. Some international ministries serving fundraising-driven expectations recruit church leaders, help them plant a church, report the results to the donors and move on to do this cycle again. These same ministries care little if that leader is trained to be sustainable. In many parts of the world heresies have been developed as western money is more concerned about ministry "results" rather than building a sustainable Christian culture.

Christian Leaders Institute, under the academic leadership of Dr. David Feddes, has been seeking to give each class the essential academics necessary that a student would get at a seminary, but in such a way that it is contextual for students everywhere.

This means that classes are put up that do not require outside books, but the equivalent of those books are given in the online syllabus. The classes include lectures that can be watched over and over again. The classes include quizzes and papers that hold students accountable to learn the material.

Dr. Feddes is now designing elective courses with legacy material that we have received recently in partnership with other ministries. The late Dr. Francis Schaeffer is being featured in one course. The late Dr. John Stott in another one. The Internet allows all of these intellectual possibilities and more.

The most important thing is that excellent intellectual ministry training is delivered while still preserving the local mentor relationship.

4. Bi-Vocational Sensitivities

We believe that most future church leaders will be bi-vocational church leaders like the Apostle Paul. The building of the training cultivation system that supports bi-vocational leaders is a passion at CLI.

CLI is very sensitive to the needs of bi-vocational leaders. We have designed courses to be very friendly for those who already have a job. The courses, while maintaining their academic rigor, can be done with students giving 2-5 hours a week. This allows a full-time working student to still receive ministry training.

The church planting action course assumes that the church planter will be bi-vocational. With funding for missions so small in this culture, church planters need to more and more have the expectation that they are going to have to support themselves in ministry until their church can afford to provide them with a salary.

5. Encouragement Culture

Rich DeVos has been a supporter of Christian Leaders Institute since the beginning. One of the points that he has made repeatedly is that in training new church leaders we are to encourage students to take their next step. He also encouraged us to give as many people the opportunity as possible and see how far their calling and dream actually take them.

Christian Leaders Institute has instituted an encourager program whereby supporters of CLI can join an encourager class and actually chat with students online. These students are from all over the world, but a CLI encourager can talk live with these students. The Internet makes all of this possible.

The encouragement that CLI encouragers bring is often the difference between staying engaged and quitting in the struggle to get their academic ministry training knowledge. I also like the encourager program because it takes many of our supporters on a "mission trip" to meet international students in lands far away.

If someone is interested in being a CLI encourager, they can check out www.christianleaders.net, where they can learn more about becoming a CLI encourager.

6. Low Ministry Overhead Oriented

The Internet is like that converter box that would change everything if it were invented. The entire school is on the Internet cloud. This is true even to the point that traditional classes are not needed. Offices are not needed. Professors are recruited and recorded. Those recordings can be used again and again. Generations of students receive training. Classes can be constantly tweaked and improved.

Christian Leaders Institute has a getting started class that is designed to replace an admissions department. If a student can get through the getting started class, they are usually able to complete all the courses at CLI. More on this class later.

The Internet has become a game-changer for ministry training. We have an opportunity as the church of God to bring excellent ministry training to support mentors and students to recruit, train and mobilize an army of called and equipped ministry leaders.

CHAPTER 3

THE VOICE OF GOD STILL CALLS

Jeremiah 1:4-5 The word of the LORD came to me, saying, "Before I formed you in the womb I knew you, before you were born I set you apart; I appointed you as a prophet to the nations."

"Called" Christian leaders are everywhere. They dwell in the slums of Ghana. They minister to people in the inner city of Baltimore. These leaders are called in the most rural places, like 100 miles from Saskatchewan, Canada. These leaders are called in places that actively persecute Christians, like Pakistan and Saudi Arabia. Called leaders are just that, called. The vast majority of these leaders do not have formal seminary training, most cannot afford it, even though that training is needed and wanted. These are the leaders that will be used by God to create long term Christian culture.

Rev. David W. Henson, Jr., of White Plains, Maryland, is one of those leaders. David has been serving as a pastor without formal training for over 26 years. He writes:

I have been married for nineteen years to my wife Connie and we live in White Plains, Maryland. I am a bi-vocational minister. When I am not serving the Lord, I work as a Service Tech for a home respiratory company. My walk with Jesus started at the age of four when my parents took me to church for the first time. I grew up with a hunger for the Word of God and I have dedicated my life to studying it. At the age of 16, I felt the call of God on my life to serve Him. After many years of studying at the School of Hard Knocks, God opened the door for me to enter the ministry. Over the past 26 years, I have had the honor of serving our Savior as an evangelist, Senior Pastor, Associate Pastor and Youth Pastor.

I remember in my younger days how much I wanted to be a famous pastor or evangelist. I wanted to travel the world for Jesus. But as I matured, I came to the realization that not all of us are called to be used that way. After serving in many capacities for His church, I understood that serving Him went way beyond my wants and desires. My goal as a minister of His glorious gospel is to be used in any way that He sees fit. He is the potter and I am the clay. I want to proclaim the love of Jesus Christ and teach people how they can be victorious in their walk of faith.

David Henson did not minister to people based on what he was going to get out of it. He sensed the call of God. He has ministered for 26 years without formal training. His calling was his ministry currency. He could never afford to get formal training despite the fact that he wanted it and needed it.

The Opportunity

What if the cultivation system for identifying, training and mobilizing Christian leaders to strengthen the church was simplified, but not compromised? What if any called leader could simply talk to their pastor, and their pastor could become their mentor or sponsor? What if high-level Bible School seminary-style education was available free of charge and brought directly to leaders through an Internet connection? What if the system was set up in such a way that strong accountability pieces were hard-wired into the process, so that those who sense the call could be tested in that call? What if the cost to develop all of this was so efficient that we could offer advanced training as a mission where contributions were not lost in residency overhead or in paying tenured professors? What if instead, for a fraction of the cost of traditional Bible schools or seminaries, you could train thousands of called Christian leaders?

Christian Leaders Institute has made major steps in bringing high-level ministry training to called leaders everywhere. This new paradigm for training called leaders has worked. From its beginning with six applications and three active students in 2006, all from the USA, Christian Leaders Institute has grown to an active student body of over 1,200 students, from all over the world. This includes the 14,000 students who applied and were accepted in the 2011-2012 school year.

Getting Started Class

Christian Leaders Institute has a getting started class that allows anyone to explore their calling and test their resolve to receive ministry training. I am going to talk more later about the thinking that goes behind the getting started class. Let me just briefly introduce this class to you.

The first part of the class introduces to students a reproducible walk with God that is the foundation for their ministry readiness. This class is positioned to be a very cost-effective admissions department. If a student can complete this part of the class, Christian Leaders Institute is more assured that these students warrant a scholarship to continue their advanced training. In this part of the class, they are invited to finish a donor profile and are granted a tuition scholarship. Students and supporting churches are asked to make donations to the school each semester they study at CLI. Supporters of this concept have enjoyed a great ministry return for their stewardship.

The second part of the class lays out the Christian basics. This is a Christian doctrine class that covers subjects like, the Bible, God, Father, Son and Holy Spirit, Sin, Salvation and much more. When the student completes these two parts of the getting started class they receive the "Christian Basics Certificate." This certificate gives them a good foundation for studying at Christian Leaders Institute.

Students will also find out after taking this getting started class whether the core basics of ministry are right for them. One of the biggest gifts Christian Leaders Institute can give is to weed out those who are not called to be pastors. This getting started class can really help students get a good start or get a good ending to their time at Christian Leaders Institute.

Equipping Called Church Leaders

Many people have asked who are the target leaders CLI is looking to recruit, train and mobilize? This question has been intensely discussed and to answer this question we had to dig deep into what is the church, what is calling, and what are characteristics and qualifications of calling. In the remainder of this chapter and the next one, I am going to share our thoughts about who Christian Leaders is looking to train.

At Christian Leaders Institute we are all about helping the called one become the sent ones!

The English word "church" comes from the Greek word "EKKLESIA." In ancient Greek that means "called out." It was clear that this word refers to people who were asked to respond to the call of the message. These believers were called to put their faith in Jesus Christ as the Messiah (John 1:41) and the Lord (I Corinthians 1:2) of their lives.

Church leaders themselves were called to put their belief, trust, and faith in Jesus as the seed of all their leadership. Pastors and church leaders cannot lead where they have not been, and definitely should not be, in ministry. The starting point is the actual call to faith, responding to the call of the gospel. If church leaders do not believe that Christ is their passion, they will be ineffective in proclaiming the gospel message and calling others into a relationship with Christ.

The calling of church leaders includes higher expectations for living out the faith and greater responsibility, despite the fact that humans are flawed and sinners. A real walk of faith is foundational if someone senses the call into ministry. This is why the ordination of church leaders has also been done prayerfully and thoughtfully. The Bible cautions against being too hasty in the ordaining of office bearers, 1 Timothy 5:22 says, "Do not be hasty in the laying on of hands, and do not share in the sins of others. Keep yourself pure."

Church leaders have a calling by Christ to intentionally order part of their time, actions, and priorities around building the ecclesia, the church.

The office of elder and deacon was instituted in the early church. The office of elder and deacon is the foundation of all leadership in the church of Christ. Out of this leadership structure bi-vocational leaders emerge. If someone would not be a worthy elder or deacon, they ought to be very wary about considering a calling into ministry. This is why Christian Leaders Institute puts a premium on local connection, mentorship and sponsorship, so that if someone senses the call into ministry, local church members, leaders and others have seen the truth of their walk and faith. If at a local level, prospective students do not have the confidence of their faith community, those students may want to seriously consider whether God has called them into church ministry.

The truth is that pastors, church planters, and chaplains all fit into the categories of elder and deacon. If prospective future church leaders have the confidence of their local bodies, and they prayerfully sense the calling to be church leaders, the local church should do all it can to train and mobilize those who are called. These called leaders will sustain Christian culture and create more capital.

Let us talk about what goes into knowing whether or not students are called into ministry. What goes into finding out if they are called to be ministry leaders? Here are seven areas of spiritual practice, as well as discernment insights, that may help students sense the calling of God to lead in ministry. No one is strong in every area, and many of these areas can be developed and cultivated in a person if they are motivated. The Apostle Paul exhibited for all time the characteristic of being a "called" church leader.

Characteristics of Called Leaders

Christian Leaders Institute is not just some high technology place where we put classes on the Internet. We are very concerned that everyone who enrolls gets a great ministry training. We also hold to the value that everyone who comes to CLI may be called to further ministry. We want called leaders who have counted the cost. Students, donors and supporters keep asking, what type of student do you seek to serve? What are the characteristics of the students you desire at Christian Leaders Institute? What qualifications are you asking of your students. I think those are great questions, and so important that I think we should talk about them.

Here are some of the characteristics of church leaders, whether bi-vocational or vocational. Prospective pastors and leaders need to read these characteristics carefully and prayerfully, in consultation with their spouses, mentors, or pastors. As they consider whether they are "called" to be a pastor, church planter or in any other ministry calling, these are the areas they will want to explore, in addition to the humble walk with God that all believers are called to embody.

While it is difficult to discern whether or not you are called by God into ministry, at Christian Leaders Institute we want new students to consider these characteristics. In the next chapter, we are going to talk about qualifications. If you are a donor or encourager of Christian Leaders Institute, you will be made more aware of what we are looking for in the called leaders that we are seeking to equip.

Vital Walk with God-inspired Call

First of all, as mentioned earlier, if future leaders are even considering being in ministry, they must have a real walk with God. And out of that walk the "call" and urgency come to them by God. Do they find themselves praying and meditating in his Word regularly? If these potentially called leaders do not care for talking to God or hearing from his Word, they should consider doing something else with their time. Being a church leader is about serving and having a relationship with God. Do they find in their prayer and devotional life that God has placed urgency in their heart for reaching others and helping others reach others? Are these leaders filled with the Holy Spirit?

The apostle Paul often talked about that urgency. He begins his epistle to the Romans,

> *Paul, a servant of Christ Jesus, called to be an apostle and set apart for the gospel of God... (Romans 1:1)*

God still calls people to call others to become leaders of the called community, the church.

Giftedness

Do future leaders have gifts or the potential of developing gifts for being ministry leaders? These prospective leaders should already have some gifts in this area, whether they are an introvert or extrovert. There are many places for ministry service in the Church of Christ.

For instance, some students desire to be church planters. A church planter directly plants culture. When someone plants a new church they really plant new culture. Do these potential leaders have gifts for church planting? Are they gifted in starting new organizations? Do they have the gift of self-aware thinking?

These and more are some of the gifts they will need to evaluate where they fit in the "called community." Gifts and competencies cannot be confused. Some may have special gifting in certain areas, but will still need to develop minimal skill in other areas. Leaders can develop competencies in areas that they are not strongly gifted in, and they can grow in areas that they are gifted in. Called leaders do amazing things with or without the complete gift package. They can mobilize and create a stage for others to use their gifts. The apostle Paul made the point that each of us has been given different gifts in the mission.

> *It was he who gave some to be apostles, some to be prophets, some to be evangelists, and some to be pastors and teachers, (Ephesians 4:11)*

Interest

Church leaders know they are called when they are actually interested in the work of the church. Is their life, breath, and love all for building the body of Christ? As they go about their day, do they find themselves thinking of ways to include people in worship, to reach people, to minister to their family and to share God's Word wherever they go? This may seem like an obvious point to make, but it is important as the leader in the church to have this genuine interest in the things of God's church. If this interest is not there, a person may not be called to ministry.

At Christian Leaders Institute, we deal with a lot of church leader types, and we have been involved in planting and pastoring lots of churches. We have noticed that called leaders have urgency about them, similar to what we hear the apostle Paul speaking of in Romans. This interest is vital to a call into church leadership.

> *I will not venture to speak of anything except what Christ has accomplished through me in leading the Gentiles to obey God by what I have said and done — by the power of signs and miracles, through the power of the Spirit. So from Jerusalem all the way around to Illyricum, I have fully proclaimed the gospel of Christ. It has always been my ambition to preach the gospel where Christ was not known,*

so that I would not be building on someone else's foundation. (Romans 15:19-20)

Temperament

Future church leaders need temperaments for leadership in the church. Do they deal with failure well? Are they leaders of peace? Church leaders have huge responsibility in the eternal destinies of souls. Will they be able to handle the stress or crack under pressure? People will criticize them. They can easily get caught up into conflicts with those they are calling to faith. Could they learn to deal with their congregation in a compassionate and understanding way?

Over the years we have been tested repeatedly. When we first went into ministry, we were figuring out who we were as leaders. Some prospective leaders have already figured much out about this, while others have much to learn. There will be much testing along the way. Church leaders have a temperament of growing when tested. Truly the apostle Paul had that temperament,

> *But we have this treasure in jars of clay to show that this all-surpassing power is from God and not from us. We are hard pressed on every side, but not crushed; perplexed, but not in despair;*

persecuted, but not abandoned; struck down, but not destroyed. We always carry around in our body the death of Jesus, so that the life of Jesus may also be revealed in our body. (2 Corinthians 4:7-10)

Humanity

Church leaders are human and they must always identify with their humanity. Some may wonder what is meant by this in relationship to calling into ministry? Are prospective leaders approachable? Are they interesting? Do they read, browse, watch interesting stuff, which many people they are called to reach interact with? For instance, they might be fans of American football. This ability, to connect with things that people do, will be important for their relating. There are so many honorable things that leaders will hold in common with their parishioners. A prospective Christian leader needs to be relatable in enough ways for them to connect to real people. Church leaders should not come off as boring or irrelevant, instead they should see everything they do as somehow tying into the calling to call people to put their faith in Christ. Church leaders are fun, they have a sense of humor, but their humor does not put people down. They can laugh at themselves and do not take themselves too seriously. They can have deep conversations but also enjoy the lighthearted side of things. Church leaders are not afraid to be real; they are open, and people can actually get to know them. They share the truth of their humanity, so that even that humanity itself can serve to lead people to walk with God.

The apostle Paul understood how to be like the people he was reaching, and then became like them. In a striking passage, Paul talks about the osmosis of what occurs when a church leader is connected to his church -- notice how human this is:

> I plead with you, brothers, become like me, for I became like you. You have done me no wrong. As you know, it was because of an illness that I first preached the gospel to you. Even though my illness was a trial to you, you did not treat me with contempt or scorn. Instead, you welcomed me as if I were an angel of God, as if I were Christ Jesus himself. (Galatians 4:12-14)

Competency of Lifestyle

Called church leaders are sustainable. Are they basically stable as people? Do they do what they say they will do? Are they truthful? Are they moderate in their life choices? Do they have healthy habits? Do they take care of themselves? Are they hurting about something from their past that still spills over in a major way? Are they bitter about something? They should be sustainable and happy with who they are, where they have been, what they are doing, and where they are going.

The apostle Paul was a very interesting man who was very competent. He supported his ministry by making tents, and he still had time to preach, teach, and heavily contribute to the starting of the Christian movement. In fact, at times his stressing of competency was so strong, people today can misunderstand the apostle Paul.

> For even when we were with you, we gave you this rule: "If a man will not work, he shall not eat." (2 Thessalonians 3:10)

Confirmation

If someone is called into ministry they should have confirmation. They should talk to those who know them best -- their spouse, family, and friends -- about whether or not they could see them as a sustainable church leader. Not having their spouse and family behind them in ministry is a red flag.

It has been said, in the calling of pastors and church planters, that there is an internal call and an external call. The internal call comes out of one's personal piety and walk with God; it includes self-assessment of whether one is called to be in ministry. The external call is others saying that a person is someone who they would hypothetically follow in the calling to faith. The apostle Paul talks about Timothy and often mentions his external calling to ministry,

> *But you know that Timothy has proved*
> *himself, because as a son with his father he*
> *has served with me in the work of the*
> *gospel. (Philippians 2:22)*

Assessing Leaders at Christian Leaders Institute

The calling of God is a work of God-believers. God has built and sustained His church for over 2000 years identifying church leaders this way. It is true that people have misread this calling, they have run from this calling and they have soiled this calling, but this is the way it has been and the universal church is the oldest organization in the world today.

Christian Leaders Institute wants to take away every unnecessary barrier from their prospective ministry candidates. The internal and external calling and all the dynamics associated with that have brought leaders from every nation and tribe ready to be trained for ministry. We want to make their training available and accessible so that hundreds of thousands of leaders are trained for the mission.

You might be reading this book wondering whether you are called into ministry? You might know someone who has mentioned an interest in looking into ministry. We have put together an exercise that will help you or someone you know determine whether a calling is possible. You or the person you know who is interested in ministry should do this exercise with as many people in a local context as possible, but do not pick too many naysayers. (Note: If someone's spouse is a naysayer that will really challenge your ability to lead in ministry) These questions can be done by you or bring them to your friend who has an interest in ministry.

Calling Assessment Exercise

Do you see in me a vital walk or the potential for a vital walk with God?

Do I possess leadership gifts? Would I be able to bless you at a church that I am thinking about starting or giving leadership in?

Do you see in me communication and interpersonal relationship skills that you would find desirable in a leader you would be associated with?

Do you see that I have the hunger for reaching people? Do you see me as on-fire to proclaim the gospel?

Do you see that I really have an interest in reaching people to the point that I would do it for free?

Do you see me as having the temperament of a church leader who will be criticized and not become bitter because of failure and challenges?

Do you see me as someone who is a person of peace who will help others grow?

Do you see me as someone who can take some risks for God?

Do you see me as approachable? Do you see me as open and willing to share?

Do you see me as someone you can relate to?

Do you see me as someone who is stable?

Do you see me as someone who is able to be sustainable as a person and as a leader of others?

Do you affirm that I have a special calling on my life for ministry?

This is not an institution where professional clergy go to get training for a high-paying job. This is where ordinary leaders can explore their ministry callings and get the necessary advanced training to do well in ministry.

If you are reading this book as a student, prayerfully consider your calling. In the next chapter, I am going to talk about the qualifications you need to aspire to in becoming a pastor or church leader.

If you are a donor or an encourager of Christian Leaders Institute, you will engage in learning about our struggle, passion and thoughtful response to the call to equip called Christian leaders for the strengthening of the church.

"Calling" really is the currency of creating a legacy of ministry like Judson, or like Hudson Taylor, or like Charles Spurgeon. At Christian Leaders Institute, If Christian leaders are called into ministry, we want to help them get the training they need to do well. This will build the kingdom of God. As you consider CLI, consider that calling into ministry has always been the key issue. Ministry leaders are not at heart rent-a-pastors; God calls them into a most holy calling.

CHAPTER 4

QUALIFIED AND READY

<u>2 Timothy 2:15</u> Do your best to present yourself to God as one approved, a workman who does not need to be ashamed and who correctly handles the word of truth.

Ann applied to be a beauty technician at a high-end salon. Even though Ann had just graduated from Beauty College and her prospects for getting the position seemed small, she filled out her application and hoped for the best. Ann got the job. She found out that it wasn't just her hair-cutting skills that landed her the job. She got the job because she showed up at the interview fashionably dressed, hair perfect, with her make up nice and looking very beautiful.

I thought that was a little questionable that she would get the job just because she dressed and presented herself in a pretty way. I thought that her skills should be the prime reason for her to get the job. I thought about this more and realized that it does make sense.

If someone wants to be into hair, they better be a

person who people trust with their hair. How many of us will get their hair cut from someone who is messy and uncombed? We want someone who lives and looks the part to cut our hair.

The same is true for the leaders in the church. They are called to lead and they must live the role.

Church leaders have <u>to be</u> the part. If called leaders are seeking ordination, they actually need to live the part appropriate for whom they are called by God to reach. Pastors and church leaders lead people out of who they are. The qualifications of church office bearers are about describing the basic traits that reflect sustainable church leaders in every generation. These qualifications are timeless and must be taken very seriously if someone believes they are called to ministry.

Qualifications are like the beauty college applicant who gets hired because she has the "qualifications" to "minister" to the beauty needs of a certain clientele. If someone is called to be a pastor, church planter, chaplain, or church staff pastor, there are certain qualifications that accompany that calling.

Appropriate To Want to Be a Pastor

Is it appropriate to want to be ordained? That is an important question. Some will argue that wanting ordination to be a deacon, elder or pastor is not something someone should want to do. Yet the Bible encourages believers to go as far as they can in serving the Lord.

Paul says to Timothy in 1 Timothy 3:1, "Here is a trustworthy saying: If anyone sets his heart on being an overseer, he desires a noble task." If that someone is you and you sense the urgency to serve God in a great capacity, that is something you should explore.

But understand that someone who is a pastor needs to actually "be the part." We want people at Christian Leaders Institute who are the part. Let's reflect on this for a while. Understand that when leaders look at their qualifications of being a leader in the church it can be overwhelming and they could easily conclude that they are not perfect or together enough to set their hearts on being church leaders.

Leaders should not be overwhelmed, instead leaders ought to be energized in these qualifications. I will go so far to say, if these qualifications are not generally present and the leader does not want to aspire to be these qualifications, that potential leaders is not called into ministry.

Qualifications of Called Leaders

As we talk about the qualifications for being an office bearer, the first thing to realize is that some of these qualifications are very objective; some are discipleship qualifications and maturity qualifications and you will not meet these qualifications perfectly.

You may find that in certain areas you are stronger than in other areas. Yet your life must reflect that you are a real work-in-progress in your desire to be a leader in the church.

Here are the characteristics of elders and pastors as found in 1 Timothy 3:2-7.

1. Leaders Who Stay Out of Trouble

"Not arrested" is the literal Greek translation. "Not arrested" could be an objective qualification, but the key question here is how are you staying out of trouble in areas that will hurt the gospel ministry. In other words, are you keeping sinful practices away from you? Are you seeking to be well respected by your community of residence? If you have a reputation for greedy or immoral activity in your community and people can come forward presently to accuse you of shady activities, you may want to think again about being a pastor. This is not to say that you may have struggled in the past and you are forever barred from ministry, just that your past needs to be addressed. Christian leaders who have gone through divorce need to have repented of any sin involved with the divorce and been restored into a healthy walk with God before they should consider being a pastor or leader in the church.

2. Leaders Who Do Not Practice Polygamy

Polygamy was practiced in Bible times and it was present in the early church. Polygamy was practiced by many of the converts from Judaism especially the wealthy. And while these new converts to Christianity may have continued to practice polygamy, office bearers and pastors were disqualified for participating in this practice. We don't know all the reasons why this was included as an objective qualification, but it was. Both elders and deacons were to "be the husband of but one wife" This is not referring here to those who have been restored after a divorce or death of a spouse and now are remarried. This is referring to polygamy.

3. Leaders Who Are Sober or Temperate in Attitude

This qualification is not talking about drunkenness; that topic is still to come. This qualification has to do with judgment. Are you circumspect in your reasoning? Are you balanced in how you evaluate yourself and others? If you "always" jump to conclusions, if you are "too positive or too negative", that is something you want to beware of as you learn ways to be more balanced.

4. Leaders Who Exhibit Moderation

The Greek word in this qualification literally means, "safe mind." Leaders who exhibit this qualification are self-controlled in their actions, opinions and speech. These leaders realize that they need to hold their counsel at times. In their personal life, they need to keep their sinful nature surrendered to Christ, understanding that they too are not perfect. Leaders like this enjoy life, but to the point that any one thing in creation does not own them other than Christ.

5. Leaders Who Act Orderly and Respectable

The Greek word here comes from the word Kosmos which means literally "order." Christian leaders who are called into the pastorate have that certain orderly and respectable trait to them. For instance, are you on time or are you habitually late to meetings? Is your dress appropriate for those that you are called to reach? Do people respect your opinion?

6. Leaders Who Are Friendly to Everyone

This Greek word is a combination of two words. The first word, filos, means friend. The second word means people, strangers, foreigners. Leaders called into the ministry are friendly and welcoming to people that are currently not part of the group. Many times this is considered by some to not be as important a character trait, yet this has everything to do with character. Hospitality is about showing someone love... even someone you do not know.

7. Leaders Who Are Willing to Teach or Mentor

Many times leaders think that this refers to teaching or preaching at a program or a worship service. There are lots of ways to teach or mentor. Church leaders see the need to pass on the lifestyle and the faith of Christianity. If you are called to be a pastor, this qualification very much applies to you. If you are a preacher you will take this very seriously in your calling. This qualification means that you will always be walking with God, learning his Word and sharing what your walk and learning brings to others

8. Leaders Who Are Not Given to Addictions

This Greek word specifically talks about "wine," literally "not near wine," referring to drunkenness. This also needs to be taken metaphorically as well. Pastors and church planters have to stay away from addictive behavior. This is challenging because addictive behavior comes in many sizes and colors. Many pastors have struggled over the centuries with various addictions. It seems like the evil one attacks in this area ferociously. The common addictions today have a lot to do with what technology brings into society. Many leaders are addicted to entertainment, video games, pornography, Internet browsing. Other leaders have struggled with substance abuse, using wine, beer and even drugs. Addictions can be food, shopping, clothing, etc. In the area of addictions, future pastors and leaders have to take this very seriously and set up accountability and support so that they are not mastered by sin or anything else in God's creation. Remember 1 Corinthians 6:12, "'Everything is permissible for me' — but not everything is beneficial. 'Everything is permissible for me' — but I will not be mastered by anything."

9. Leaders Who Are Not Violent

This Greek word literally means "not a striker." It means someone who is not given to violent outbursts or angry blasts. Pastors and leaders are not given to revenge or payback. Hate and anger are not the operating system of a pastoral personality. Have you ever seen a pastor or leader exhibit a violent outrage? This outrage will bring harm to their ministry more than it will make some point to the person they offended.

10. Leaders Who Are Not Greedy Misers

The literal meaning of the Greek word here is base or selfish gain. In other words, leaders who are solely motivated by what they get financially or in other forms of repayment are not qualified to be pastors. While the apostle Paul writes that the worker deserves his wages, there is a fine line here between career and calling. You should not become a pastor because you think it is a nice job where you will get paid well. This is a calling and you cannot think of this calling as a career. Instead, you are to be motivated out of generosity and realize that God will cover all your needs as you are a good steward of what He gives you.

11. Leaders Who Are Self-Aware in Their Gentleness

The Greek word here is "appropriate." By implication this word is translated as gentle, mild, or patient. We need to add one more dimension to that word and that dimension is self-awareness in your responses. In every relationship and in every church things will happen and maybe even offensive words will be said to you. Many times someone will treat the pastor in a way that gives the pastor a clue of what is needed. For instance, if someone is unfairly critical of the pastor, this is likely how he treats his family. This gives you great insight in to how to give pastoral care to that family and that person. Remember the axiom, how someone treats you is how he likely treats others in his life.

12. Leaders Who Love Peace

Some people have to win every fight and be right about every issue. This does not a good pastor make. While some fights are very important to win, most fights are not worth the time to get involved with. The apostle Paul encourages us to live at peace with others. He writes in Romans 12:18, "If it is possible, as far as it depends on you, live at peace with everyone."

As a called pastor, you must be very careful as you lead people to peace. Some pastors exert control to bring unity on an issue by telling parishioners that God has led them to this opinion or position. Be very care about leading as an ambassador of God, that you really want peace not the appearance of peace.

13. Leaders Who Are Not Covetous

This is a "killer" in ministry. The Greek word here means "wishing for more silver." It refers to a lot of thoughts and desires that will sink your ministry calling. The fact is that you will never have enough money. You will never have the perfect church, you will never have the perfect family or spouse. Where you are now may not be as good as where you were a year ago. Imagining that the future may be better than now may not help you. Effective Christian leaders are content even while they are seeking to improve. Called leaders are to be content in who they are and where they are. It is from that contentment that they can determine if they should take another church or do something else. They are not motivated by the grass is greener over there attitude. Whether it is with silver or something else, effective pastors are content in Christ.

14. Leaders who Lead in Their Homes and Are Respected

The issues of leadership are a microcosm of the issues of leadership in any church setting. If you are able to give appropriate leadership in your family, including your spouse, this will directly translate in the church.

If your children do not see in you that you are a Biblical leader who commands respect, people outside your family will have a hard time seeing that as well. All the issues of your leadership have a foundation in your family. Someone's reputation in their family is huge in how they will be received in the church. The apostle Paul even quips, "(If anyone does not know how to manage his own family, how can he take care of God's church?)" (1 Timothy 3:5)

15. Leaders Who are Settled in Their Walk and Doctrine

The apostle Paul observed many early leaders that fell away from the faith. If you are called into ministry you want to be settled in your walk and in your doctrine. Paul writes in 1 Timothy 3:6, "He must not be a recent convert, or he may become conceited and fall under the same judgment as the devil." When you are unsettled in your walk or doctrine what happens is you are open for attitudes and ideas that leave the Biblical worldview.

If you or your spouse are a recent convert, go slowly into pursuing your ministry calling. Later in 1 Timothy 3, the apostle Paul encourages that deacons be tested. "They must keep hold of the deep truths of the faith with a clear conscience. They must first be tested; and then if there is nothing against them, let them serve as deacons." (1 Timothy 3:9-10)

Leaders need to be tested. Where have you been tested? How have you done? What did you learn?

16. Leaders Who Are Respected in Their Community of Relationships

The same principle applies here that applies with a leader's family. If someone is interacting with people and they see that that leader is fair and honest, this says a lot about whether that person could be qualified to be a pastor. On the other hand, if the community has experienced that the leader treats people badly this says a lot about whether the person is ready to be a pastor or church leader.

Assessment

If you are a new or potential student at Christian Leaders Institute, I want you to prayerfully read each of these 15 qualifications and to develop an honest assessment of where you are now. Then I encourage your to develop a plan to grow in these qualifications. You will never be perfect, but a teachable attitude led by God's grace, His Word and Spirit will transform you into a Christian leader who will be used by God to change the world. Have your spouse, mentor, sponsor or trusted friend, go over each one of these qualifications with you. Aspire to BE these qualifications.

.

Ordination and Christian Leaders Institute

Thousands of Christian Leaders Institute students have been seeking ordination. These students have varied understandings of what ordination means. CLI students come from various traditions and have various understandings of many topics concerning ordination, such as: Who can be ordained? What roles can women be ordained into? How does someone get ordained?

Christian Leaders Institute recognizes that we are training Christian leaders and giving them the best possible ministry training so that they can minister in their local context. This does mean that our professors will share their scriptural convictions guided by our Statement of Faith. We recognize that there will not be complete agreement about many issues including tongues, end times, and ordinations. We are going to look at the basic Biblical and practical insights that inform those who are sensing the call to ministry and ordination.

What is Ordination?

The definition of ordination is different for those in different church traditions. Ordination to the Catholics, Anglicans, Methodists, Lutherans and other high ordination denominations is primarily connected to Christian leaders already in place. These leaders appoint new leaders who have demonstrated calling, gifts and competency. Ordination to Presbyterians and Reformed denominations are much more connected to elder assemblies. Ordination in the Baptist, Assemblies,

Congregational, non-denominational, house church movement and other more grass-roots authority traditions see ordination as coming out of the democratic structure of the authority of the group. Ordination to many is defined as a certificate of ordination like a certificate of certification that some organizations give leaders for their credibility.

Christian Leaders Institute Goals

Christian Leaders Institute seeks to equip called leaders to be ready for their ordination. If they already are ordained, our goal is to better equip them for effective service in their ministry position. We have a "bloom where you are planted" approach to training Christian leaders. Leaders come to us with a calling to minister, our goal is to help them get ready.

The last two chapters dealt with the "who" of the leaders we seek to train at Christian Leaders Institute. Being a church leader is being a called leader who has the qualifications to honorably discharge the duties of one of God's servants. We are looking for leaders whose calling and qualifications converge together to characterize the leaders who will proclaim the gospel. While no one is perfect in every way, called and qualified leaders are the ones Christian Leaders Institute seek to train.

If you are reading this book as a student and the last two chapters substantially characterize you, we welcome you to start your training at Christian Leaders Institute. If you are an encourager to students, you are now aware of who these church leaders are aspiring to be in their training and preparedness for ministry. If you are a donor, you can see that your donations are not just about paying for ministry training; CLI takes each leader's calling, character, and qualifications very seriously.

Christian Leaders Institute is looking to train called ministry leaders who embody the characteristics of inspiring leaders. We are also seeking to train qualified leaders who are the part. These goals of assessment can be difficult to accomplish and we are convinced that we will not do it as well as we want to, but we will keep adjusting our program and working toward effectively identifying, training and mobilizing called Christian leaders. In the next chapter, we are going to look at how the Getting Started Class is a great introduction to ministry training and a test that separates the called from those that are just checking ministry training out.

CHAPTER 5

GETTING STARTED AT CHRISTIAN LEADERS INSTITUTE

> 2 Peter 1:2-3 Grace and peace be yours in abundance through the knowledge of God and of Jesus our Lord. His divine power has given us everything we need for life and godliness through our knowledge of him who called us by his own glory and goodness.

When I was visiting Kenya, Africa in the year 2000, I happened on a newspaper, and I noticed that many young people were dying of AIDS. I expressed my sadness that this terrible sexually transmitted disease was ravishing so many young people, whether they were Christians or non-Christians. I asked a local Christian leader his opinion about this tragedy. He gave me a history lesson I have never forgotten.

I don't remember the various dates he mentioned, but I remember that he said when the missionaries from the developing western nations came to evangelize, they were connected to money, power, and medicine. As they proclaimed the gospel it was very hard to separate the claims of the gospel from the expectations of the imperial nations that controlled the land. For instance, to be a Christian meant certain western expectations of modest clothing accompanied conversion. To be a Christian included dietary issues. Many higher western hymns replaced the indigenous sounds of the native land.

The result was that many Christians had a hard time distinguishing the root of gospel faith from the fruits of gospel faith. In other words, the call of faith was so culturally wrapped up. Over time to be "Christian" was a whole package of behaviors or morality and the core relationship and doctrines were replaced with religion and behaviors.

But what does AIDS have to do with fruit and root confusion? That Christian leader in Kenya said that the message many in his country reproduced over generations was a very shallow faith that did little to really restrain sensual indulgence. He went on to say that Christianity was the "breast cover up" religion but not the faith that changes hearts. With hearts unchanged, sensual indulgence was not put in check. So-called "Christians" were just as immoral as non-Christians, they were just more outwardly modest.

This really made me think. When we proclaim the call to faith, are we proclaiming the gospel that changes humans at the root level, that is their hearts? Or are we proclaiming a gospel that changes social structures, so that at the end of the day we confuse the call of the gospel faith? I want to be very clear here that I do believe that the call of the gospel in the hearts of believers will have powerful fruit that will change culture, but we all have to be clear about what the root is and what the fruits are. We have to be very clear about what we are proclaiming as we introduce the call of faith.

What are you called to proclaim? You are called to proclaim the gospel. Those that hear and believe will be saved and are part of the family of God. Church leaders lead or form a "hear the call-to-faith organization," this organization is called the church. The church leader is calling people to believe the message that will change their destiny. When people respond to the message with faith, they are actually born again. Even the faith itself comes from hearing the message. *"Consequently, faith comes from hearing the message, and the message is heard through the word of Christ." (Romans 10:17)*

Church leaders are asking people to put their faith in Christ as their Lord and Savior. They are asking people to be God-centric and not man-centric. They are asking people to order their entire lives around their walk with God, guided by his Word. They are asking people to submit themselves to God and each other as the Bible encourages and commands.

Recently, I received a note from one of our African students. He writes about the misconceptions that Africans have about God. What fascinated me about this note is that many Africans have come to believe that all religions are the same. I would venture to say that most people think that religions are about rules and morality, but this student got it right. It has always been about a heart connected to the Father through Jesus. Here was what Moses wrote me:

> Hi Henry,
>
> In the country where I live, some people have a lot of misconceptions about God, the role and personality of Jesus. It's unfortunate that many even do not see the difference between Rastafarianism, Islam, Christianity, and the African Traditional Religion among others. It's common to hear people say that 'all roads lead to Rome,' meaning that all religions lead to heaven/God, but I believe that no one gets to the Father except through Jesus Christ.

Church leaders are going after the heart, the will, and the soul to restore humans into a forgiven relationship with Christ, won for us by the sacrifice of Christ on the cross and the victory of Christ over death in Christ's resurrection. They are asking hearts to believe in Jesus as their Lord and Savior. *"Therefore, holy brothers, who share in the heavenly calling, <u>fix</u> your thoughts on Jesus, the apostle and high priest whom we confess." (Hebrews 3:1) "For the message of the cross is foolishness to those who are perishing, but to us who are being saved it is the power of God." (1 Corinthians 1:18)*

Church leaders need to be very careful to proclaim the root of faith and then call people to the faith that changes hearts from the inside out. Over the years, I have found that I have always needed to be clear about what we are actually asking people to get themselves into when they enter a relationship with Christ. What is the root?

At Christian Leaders Institute we believe the root is a living relationship with God -- Father, Son, and Holy Spirit. We are very careful about laying the foundation for the "knowledge of God.' We are not giving people merely "Religious Training."

At Christian Leaders Institute we have a getting started procedure that deals with the two key understandings of someone's knowledge of God. Knowledge of God is relational knowledge that includes what we call walking with God. This walking includes prayer and devotional Bible reading and the habits that are associated with that daily walk. This relationship walk is to be reproducible through evangelism.

There is also another kind of knowing of God that is included in "walking" with God, this is the doctrinal knowledge. Both these types of knowing God are very important. At Christian Leaders Institute, this two part class is the foundational class that students take that launches them into the rest of their ministry training. This chapter will help you see the DNA of Christian Leaders Institute's foundational Getting Started Class. Knowing God through a relational walking is the first part of the class, and the second part of the class is knowing God in a doctrinal way.

As we plant or support Christianity worldwide, we have to be very clear that we build on the root of the gospel and do not promote the fruit as the essence of our faith. The fruit of the faith comes out of the root. We have a Getting Started Class that seeks to help students start their education on the foundation of the walk and thought of the knowledge of God. Let me show you now in more detail how the Getting Started Class works.

Welcome Aboard

Called leaders from around the world find out about Christian Leaders Institute from many sources, including organic optimization, Google Ads, Internet or organizational referrals and word of mouth. They go to our website and fill out an application for enrollment. They are placed into the Getting Started Class.

The Getting Started Class functions to give anyone the opportunity to explore whether they are candidates for ministry training at Christian Leaders Institute. Our goal is that ten to twenty percent will finish this class and move on becoming active students earning certificates and diploma. This class replaces the overhead of an admissions department and eliminates those who are not serious or able to study at Christian Leaders Institute.

The class is divided into two parts and a student will be awarded 7 credits and will received the Christian Basics Certificate when they complete the class.

Features of the Two-Part Getting Started Class

The getting started class is divided into two parts. There are several features of the getting started class that form the DNA of the Christian Leaders Institute curriculum.

Let me show you what each part of the getting started class seeks to accomplish. These six characteristics of the getting started class give our students a great start!

1. Important Walk with God and Doctrinal Orientation

First Part of the Getting Started Class:

In this first part of the class, students learn or review the essence of a walk with God. They learn about how a walk with God includes reproducibly talking to God (prayer) and listening to God (Bible reading) in a repeated way. Students learn these reproducible faith-formation habits and how to share them in evangelism.

These habits are taught to students in the Seven Connections, which outline a reproducible walk with God which includes the student's personal life, marriage, family, friends, church service, kingdom and world. These seven connections really are the places where spiritual capital is built which builds a Christian culture.

Lectures in video format are shared with students. The students take quizzes that are automatically graded to make sure that they actually engage with the materials. Our internet tools notice whether the students actually even read the materials and watch the videos.

Second Part of the Getting Started Class:

The second part of the class features the teachings of Dr. Ed Roels. Dr. Roels has not only been the president of Kuyper College, a pastor in a local church, and an executive leader at the Bible League, he is a skilled theological communicator. Dr. David Feddes, our provost, has taken Dr. Roels' Christian Basics material and created a class including video lectures that lays an excellent foundation for the doctrines of the faith.

Students are quizzed after each topics and the topics are historic key doctrinal topics including,

The Bible
God
Creation
Jesus Christ
Salvation
The Holy Spirit
Christian Living
Suffering and Persecution
The Future

Students learn these truths and more, find where they are taught in Scripture, and grow in their ability to state Christian truths clearly and briefly to others.

2. Assures Students are Academically ready for Ministry Training.

The Getting Started Class is designed in such a way that if a student can complete these classes and pass the quizzes, they have the essential academic skills necessary to succeed at the rest of the curriculum. The class has enough intellectually-stimulating content that students are engaged in concepts both theological and practical, which introduce them to the study of ministry training.

Academic training is important. Christian Leaders Institute seeks to not just give practical ministry insights, but also intellectually-stimulating training which prepares our students to become life-long learners of intellectual insights. We tailor our classes to different learning styles. Our classes also take into account that many of our students have English as a second language. We expect that the students will take the academic training seriously.

3. Assures Students' Technology Level is Workable for Success.

This class is designed to check out the Internet connections and the technological skills of the students. Everything "technologically" that happens in the Getting Started Class tests whether the students will be able to complete the CLI program. As the Internet continues to penetrate the globe, more and more students will be able to succeed.

We have students who have high speed Internet connections even in the most remote places. Whether in rural Jamaica or urban Nairobi, Kenya, students have access to this training. In many places of the globe, students have computers and Internet before they have clean water.

The Getting Started Class teaches even the most technologically illiterate students basic computer skills. Many of the students have been taught at CLI the skills that help them do well in their country, navigating newer technology that most in their country do not have yet. CLI is often a real blessing for our students.

4. Assures that Student's Commitment Level is Acceptable.

There is nothing like these two substantial parts of a class that tests whether someone is serious about their ministry calling. This Getting Started Class weeds out those students who really want ministry training from those who are just toying with the idea. This is very important in a mission that is seeking to keep expenses low. We do not want to utilize resources on those who are not called, qualified and committed to do the work needed.

We have taken great pains to make sure that the Getting Started Class tests students in their resolve. For instance, we ask students to actually develop Bible reading and prayer habits. We believe these are important practices for every pastor or Christian leader.

5. Introduces the Culture of Christian Leaders Institute.

Students are introduced to the staff of Christian Leaders Institute via video. Students are introduced to the culture of CLI. Many frequently asked questions are raised and answered in these classes. There are videos that explain the curriculum and videos that explain the admissions process.

Students are introduced to the global identity of Christian Leaders Institute. They find out about our "Chat" feature whereby students can talk to each other. Students are introduced to opportunities to make a donation to Christian Leaders Institute. When a student completes the Getting Started Class, they have connected with the curriculum, some professors, chatting, and giving.

6. Connects Students with the Culture of Support

As students complete their Getting Started Class they are required to develop a student profile. This profile includes their story and their ministry dream. This profile is used to share with donors and supporters to engage churches and future churches who are benefiting from their support. These profiles are so encouraging and are shared on the Web as encouragement to everyone who comes in contact with Christian Leaders Institute.

We really encourage our students to communicate who they are so that we can support those who support Christian Leaders Institute. We have found the students willing and ready to share their lives with encouragers and donors.

The Getting Started Classes has been a work in progress for many years. For the last several years, we have been tweaking this class, making it better and better. The Getting Started Class is still a work in progress as we seek to include as many called leaders as possible.

CHAPTER 6

ON-LINE CURRICULUM FOR MINISTRY TRAINING

The year was 96 AD. Christianity appeared in jeopardy. Sixty-three years had passed since Jesus rose from the dead. Thirty years had passed since Nero killed the apostles Paul and Peter. The personal qualities of the first leaders were fading. New leaders were being identified and mobilized. Would Christianity thrive? What would these new leaders be taught? While they had the writings of the Old Testament and the writings of the apostles, what would be the organizing curriculum that would train the leaders? What would be the content of the teaching that would lead the people to form a new and deepening Christian capital that would eventually change society itself?

The church had as its foundational spiritual capital an inspired Old and New Testament (though complete agreement on all the books that were to be included in this "canon" would be hashed out over the next 200 years). This canon itself would communicate the walk with God that would be passed down from generation after generation up to today.

Snapshot in Time of a Reproducible Christian Culture

In 96 AD, the apostolic age was over. How would the church survive? What were the essentials that needed to be passed to the next generation? It was in this backdrop that Clement of Rome penned an epistle to the Corinthian church. The church of Corinth was struggling. Clement of Rome was asked to speak into the conflict.

He contextualized in a clear way the reproducible culture of the church that made up Christianity for generations. He opened his epistle complimenting the culture of Christianity that was alive in Corinth. When we look at training ministry leaders today at CLI, we have this inspiration to create a curriculum that builds gospel capital today like it did in the time of Clement. As you read what Clement wrote in 96 AD, you will see how relevant his words are for developing a curriculum to meet the needs of today's Christian leaders.

Clement of Rome opened up his epistle to the Corinthians this way:

> "For who ever dwelt even for a short time among you, and did not find your faith to be as fruitful of

virtue as it was firmly established? Who did not admire the sobriety and moderation of your godliness in Christ? Who did not proclaim the magnificence of your habitual hospitality? And who did not rejoice over your perfect and well-grounded knowledge? For you did all things without respect of persons, and walked in the commandments of God, being obedient to those who had the rule over you, and giving all fitting honor to the presbyters among you." English Translation of 1 Clement by Roberts-Donaldson

This epistle was read in Corinth and in churches throughout the Christian world. Clement had the time and distance from the actual presence of the apostles to see what was reproducible and what of Christian culture continues beyond Christian leaders' lives. His epistle addressed seven areas of Christian Culture that were challenges in 96 AD and in the same way his epistle was relevant then, it is an apt word for today.

The Challenge To Reproduce the Faith

The challenges of 96 AD are still with every church. The list that Clement of Rome put together inspires Christian Leaders Institute. You will notice this reproducible focus embedded in our classes and curriculum. Sometimes it is obvious, sometimes it is subtle, but it is always present.

What vision of reproducing Christian Culture will you see at Christian Leaders Institute? Let me go over each point that Clement of Rome made in more detail as we seek to reproduce Christian culture in a world needing Christ so urgently. We desire that Christian church leaders who graduate from Christian Leaders Institute will exhibit leadership that will bring about:

1. Faith-Called Communities

> We are training CLI students to lead in bringing faith-called communities, rooted around the gospel truth that Jesus defeated sin and death on the cross and rose victorious, sealing eternal life and relationship for those that put and keep their trust in Him.

> These faith-called communities are called to bear fruit. They are positive and have a transformative action that goes beyond the church community.

> Church leaders are called-out leaders of faith, first in their own lives. Then they can impact lives in their local church and beyond. As the leaders are called, so also the church is called to be "ecclesia."

2. Biblical Moderation Communities

> We are training CLI students to lead in bringing churches where healthy boundaries are clearly developed in applying the doctrines of the church. We are training CLI leaders to keep the divisive agenda from side-tracking the community of faith. Church leaders need to be both vitally alive in their walks with God and display balance in their personal lives in order to lead toward a sustainable, balanced community of faith.

3. Habitual Hospitality

> We are training CLI students to lead in bringing churches to become friendly welcoming places. This welcoming mentality is the engine that drives every ministry and service.

> Called church leaders and their spouses need to be welcoming people. Out of that hospitable fullness, others will be inspired to lead in their local church.

4. Biblical Doctrine

We are training CLI students to lead churches into vital and orthodox biblical and historical doctrine. If doctrine is not remaining biblical, the church will drift. Graduates of CLI are taught the essential teachings which enable them to live and proclaim sound Biblical doctrine.

The second part of the Getting Started Class on "Basic Biblical Doctrine" has been added to the curriculum. Dr. Feddes developed this class with Dr. Ed Roels. Dr. Roels was the president of Reformed Bible College. He has written training materials for many decades.

5. Ministry Inclusion

We are training CLI students to lead churches in not showing favoritism to any one group. Everyone is welcome to participate.

CLI trained leaders are not elitists. They do not create tensions between different people. Everyone is a creational image bearer of God and is worth reaching for Christ.

Even the very poor deserve excellent ministry training. We raise money making it clear that everyone who comes forward gets an opportunity to receive a quality ministry training experience.

6. Vital Piety and Walk

We are training CLI students to lead churches which encourage and support Christians to walk in vital piety with God. There are important habits of connection that fuel a faith-called community. For church leaders, those vital piety practices power both their walk and all the walks of those in their churches.

The Getting Started Class covers this important area.

7. Healthy and Fitting Leadership.

We are training CLI students to lead in their churches with a balanced, healthy leadership style that creates stages for others to use their gifts. Student will learn how to cultivate new leaders in the church. Churches will not remain if the leadership is weak. New churches can get great starts, but if their leadership cultivation system and execution is lacking, new churches will struggle or die. Existing churches need to keep recruiting and mobilizing new leaders, even encouraging leaders to become bi-vocational pastors.

The Christian Leaders Curriculum

Many have asked how did you come to the curriculum you offer at Christian Leaders Institute? This is an important question and we owe you the reasoning behind the curriculum we offer. We also want to be very clear of what the doctrinal perspective is that guides the materials that are taught.

What is a curriculum? The word curriculum means "race course." There were many around the early 1900s who really focused on what curriculums should be taught. One such man was John Franklin Bobbit. He was part of the era of Henry Ford and Dale Carnegie. This was the era of efficiency, whereby everyone was challenged to be their very best, and waste was to be eliminated. Bobbit was on a mission sent by the USA to do social engineering in the Philippines. The American leaders wanted more of the social capital of "efficiency" of that era to drive Philippine culture. A curriculum really is the teacher's "canon" of what should be taught to the next generation. Curriculums are very important.

Every curriculum is constructed out of a world-view. Another curriculum creator was John Dewey, who believed in a world without God. He believed that the "pastors" of society were the teachers in the public school. The content of this curriculum separated science from religion. John Dewey's curriculum was very centered on a community of democracy as the ideal. We can see why he is still very popular.

Curriculums form the content of what is taught by the leaders. Church leaders have as our foundation the Bible, and the Bible applies to all generations. If we look at the history of the church, we will notice that the curriculum that the leaders used did change. The early church curriculum was replaced by a tradition-laden curriculum that taught that the church organization controlled whether someone was saved or not.

New curriculums were developed at the time of the Reformation that proclaimed that people had a direct connection to God and were saved by God's grace, though faith, and supported by the church as a called body of believers. The hierarchy of the church was re-thought by the Protestants. New curriculums were written and taught to the leaders.

What makes a good curriculum? A Christian curriculum comes from a God-honoring worldview which places God's Word, the Bible, as the foundational and sole rule of life and teachings. What are the important points of Christianity? The historic doctrines of the church taught in the Ecumenical creeds like the Apostle's Creed, the Nicene Creed, and the Athanasian Creed. Since the Reformation happened, this shapes things so that the emphasis on what is taught stays focused on Scripture alone, faith alone, the priesthood of all believers, and other important doctrines.

Christian Leaders Institute
Statement of Faith

- The Bible is God's inerrant Word, the only final authority for faith and life.
  (Proverbs 30:5-6; Isaiah 8:20; John 10:35; 2 Timothy 3:16-17; 2 Peter 1:21)

- God is Trinity, an eternal, loving unity of three divine Persons: Father, Son, and Holy Spirit.
  (Deuteronomy 6:4; Matthew 28:19; John 14:26; 2 Corinthians 13:14)

- God created the universe ex nihilo, from nothing, and made all things very good.
  (Genesis 1-2; Exodus 20:11; Hebrews 11:3)

- God created humanity to glorify and enjoy God and to be stewards of creation.
  (Genesis 1:26-28; Psalm 8; Isaiah 43:7; Revelation 4:11; Psalm 37:4)

- Humanity has fallen into sin, and we are totally unable to save ourselves.
  (Genesis 3; Romans 3:12, 23; Romans 5:12)

- Jesus Christ is fully God and fully man.
  (Matthew 1:21-23; John 1:1,14; 20:28; Hebrews 1:1-4, 2:14)

- Jesus was born of a virgin, obeyed God perfectly, worked great miracles, died on a cross, rose from the dead, ascended to heaven, and reigns over all things.
  (Luke 1:26-35, Hebrews 4:15; John 14:11, Luke 23-24, Ephesians 1:20-23)

- Salvation is merited only by Jesus' perfect obedience and substitutionary atonement.
  (Isaiah 53; Hebrews 7:26-27; 2 Corinthians 5:21; Acts 4:12)

- Salvation is entirely God's gift, not our achievement, and is received by faith, not works.
  (John 3:16; Romans 1:16-17; Galatians 2:16-21)

- The Holy Spirit gives new birth, unites us to Christ, equips us with His gifts, and empowers us to be His ambassadors. (John 3:3-8; Romans 8:9-11; Ephesians 3:16-21; 1 Corinthians 12; Acts 1:8)

- The church is the one body of God's people

throughout all generations and from all nations.
(Romans 12:5; Galatians 3:26-29; Ephesians 1:22-23; Revelation 7:9)

- Christ gives two signs and seals of his grace:
  baptism and the Lord's Supper.
  (John 4:1; 1 Corinthians 12:13; Matthew 28:19;
  Mark 14:22-24; 1 Corinthians 11:23-26)

- God's holy angels defend and help God's people.
  (Psalm 34:7, 91:11; Matthew 18:10; Hebrews 1:14)

- Satan and other fallen angels are dangerous but doomed. Christ is victor.
  (Ephesians 6:10-18; Colossians 2:15; 1 Peter 5:8; Revelation 12:10-12)

- Christ will return visibly to rule the world and to make all things new.
  (Matthew 24:30; 1 Thessalonians 4:16; Revelation 21:1-5)

- God's people will rejoice forever in heaven; God's enemies will suffer forever in hell.
  (Daniel 12:2-3; Matthew 25:31-46; Revelation 22:1-5; 2 Thessalonians 1:9)

- God's covenant addresses not only individuals but also their families.

(Genesis 17:7; 18:19; Deuteronomy 7:9; Joshua 24;15; Psalm 103:17; Acts 11:14; 16:15,31)

- As individuals, as couples, and as families, we need daily conversation with God through Bible reading and prayer. (Psalm 1; Daniel 6:10; Deuteronomy 6:4-9; Ephesians 6:18; 1 Thessalonians 5:17)

- We are called to a life of love, as depicted in the Ten Commandments.
  (Exodus 20:1-17; Mark 12:30-31; John 14:15; Romans 13:8-10; 1 Corinthians 13)

- We are called to spread the gospel to people who don't yet follow Christ.
  (Psalm 96:3; Matthew 5:14; 28:18-20; 1 Peter 3:15)

- We are called to a world view and way of life which seeks to honor Christ in every area of thought and action. (Psalm 24:1; Colossians 3:17; 2 Corinthians 10:5)

Christian Leaders Institute takes curriculum very seriously. Our belief statement forms the core of what we believe. This belief statement was founded on Scripture and inspired by the historic church creeds of the faith, especially post-Reformation. Christian Leaders Institute is taking the ancient teachings and putting them on the web so that called future ministry leaders will be able to reproduce these teachings and a godly walk to those people God calls them to lead.

The curriculum of CLI is focused to build from and on the Christian capital of the past, addressing the critical issues that leaders face today. What is interesting to me is that I believe we are going back to themes that were very relevant in the early church. Clement of Rome was after the same thing as he addressed the Corinthians.

The Early Church and Today

I began this chapter by talking about the church in 96 AD. I am going to list what the Church in 96 AD faced and how the church today is facing similar challenges, which inspired the design of our curriculum to meet the needs of reproducing Christianity even in very hostile places.

1. Faith-Tested

The early Christians planted churches in a hostile place that tested their beliefs to the core. Around 65 AD Roman Emperor Nero persecuted Christians, blaming them for the fires that burned much of Rome. And from 91-96 AD Roman Emperor Domitian persecuted Christians because they would not acknowledge him as deity. And yet, the leaders of the church were out there testifying for the faith, sharing the gospel even to the point of being martyred.

Today: The Christian faith is being tested in various ways. Called pastors and church leaders will face the assault on the Christian message and practice daily.

- Secular philosophy taught at universities is selling evolution as the explanation for the origins of the universe.

- Many governments still persecute those who spread Christianity.

- Popular culture is generally rebellious to the existence of the God of the Bible and have proclaimed Him to be dead.

- Other religions, most notably Islam, are not tolerant of the proclamation of Christianity.

Christian Leaders Institute seeks to train leaders who are up for the challenge of spreading the faith.

2. Extreme Beliefs and Practices Erupted

Unsustainable attitudes were creeping into many churches. These attitudes had the possibility to trap the early church in extreme interpretations of their walk or obedient piety. This was not promoting the root of the faith, but getting caught up in defining the faith, taking off some aspects of Christian teaching. For example, all believed that there was a sinful nature, but two extremes developed:

- The Nicolaitans, who claimed that sinful acts committed in the flesh did not connect to a person's spiritual life. (Revelations 2:6,15)

- The Gnostics, who held that the "flesh" was evil, including even sexuality in marriage. They even had a problem with the fact that Christ himself took on human flesh. (2 John 1:7 and 1 Timothy 4:2-6)

Today: Throughout the world today, Poorly trained church leaders have been spreading unbalanced Christianity that is not Biblical.

- In America, Christians have often aligned themselves with either conservative or liberal political agendas. While biblically informed voting is good, this has confused the core message of Christianity.

- In Africa, Christianity is said to be a mile wide and an inch deep. There are places where poor ministry teaching has created churches that are more concerned with superficial practices than with a deep and abiding culture of Christianity.

- In India, name a heresy and you will find it there. Biblical ministry training is not accessible there for most called leaders.

- in the islands, the Christian leaders do not have resources to get in-depth ministry training that helps them lead their people beyond superstitious imbalances.

- Name a Place: In-depth ministry training is needed!

3. Hospitality Challenged

Hospitality practiced by early Christians included: caring for the poor, opening their homes to strangers, and bringing restorative justice to people when no one else would. But hospitality was weakening in hearts. Also, inviting strangers into homes was becoming dangerous because of persecution. The author of the book of Hebrews is very intentional about reminding the Hebrew believers not to give up meeting with each other and to remember to continue practicing hospitality even toward strangers (Hebrews 13:2). The apostle John reminded the church to continue to offer hospitality to leaders so they can effectively work for the spread of the church (3 John 1:8).

Today: Hospitality is a lost practice. This is one area that would be a game-changer, if Christians were known as the most hospitable people on earth.

Christian Leaders Institute's training highlights hospitality often in various courses, such as Church and Ministry and Church Planting.

4. False Prophets and Troublemakers Appeared

Church teachings and knowledge were challenged. Deceivers and false teachers were sidetracking believers into different unbiblical teachings. Many Christians were straying from the clear teachings of the apostles and were getting stuck in challenging the humanity and deity of Christ. The teaching of Christ's return was understood by many believers to mean that Christ would return before the end of the apostolic age. But their leaders died and Christ did not reappear. Near this time John was given the vision that formed the book of Revelations, encouraging the church that Jesus was indeed coming, but no one would or could know the hour.

Today: Whether it is the prosperity gospel, or liberal churches that no longer believe the Bible to be the inspired Word of God, false prophets are in the church and in-depth ministry training is needed.

5. Elitism

It is hard to imagine, but in the early Christian world, elitism mattered too much in some places. In the lukewarm church of Laodicea, John has this to say, "You say, 'I am rich; I have acquired wealth and do not need a thing.' But you do not realize that you are wretched, pitiful, poor, blind and naked." All people whether they have means or not are to attend and support their church (1 Timothy 6:17-18).

Showing favoritism to any person based on their status, class, race or political position has always been frowned on as not consistent with a person that walks with Christ (James 2:1;9).

Today: Ministry Training is not easy to receive. We are constantly thanked by Christian Leaders Institute students that we make ministry training accessible to everyone by giving a scholarship to everyone who believes in our statement of faith and finishes the Getting Started Class.

6. Christian Walks Weakened

The "walk" or relational connection with Christ was struggling in many places. Christianity was about a loving, zealous relationship with Christ the ascended

Lord. This "piety" included the habits of meeting together for worship, participating in the Lord's Supper, and practicing home discipleship. But this "piety" was not just rote habits. This was a loving relationship walk with God. If faith was trust in God's promises, Word, and actions, Walking with God, or piety, was about how believers really thought of or felt toward the God they served. In Laodicea, doctrine, hospitality, church government and faith were not questioned, but their walk with Christ was dull..."you are neither cold nor hot" (Revelations 3:16). The Laodiceans were indifferent in their love for God, although they may have still met for some pious habits. In Sardis, the church's walk was not only dull, but also dead. "You have a reputation of being alive, but you are dead" (Revelations 3:2). In Sardis, their habits were just a big show, but their hearts were dead toward God.

Today. This has also been a challenge. At so many levels, our daily walk with God is challenged because of time and business and thousands of other agendas. Christian Leaders Institute seeks to not only promote and spread the faith but also assure that walking with God is the foundational practice of all students (More on this later).

7. Original Leaders Were Dying and Getting Old

Church leadership problems challenged the sustainability of Christianity. New leaders were getting in place to take the church into a new era. Every apostle was dead except John, and he was exiled to the remote island of Patmos. The pioneering leaders appointed by the apostles were either dead, dying under persecution, or getting old. Factions developed between the "old" leadership appointed by the apostles and the "new" second-generation's leadership. Some churches were even deposing their existing leaders.

Today leaders are exiting the stage and new ones are needed. It appears that because of the lack of resources, most of these new leaders need to be bi-vocational. We cannot cheat these leaders out of a full and effective ministry training program.

The goal of the curriculum at Christian Leaders Institute is to reproduce healthy and vital Christianity building on the already existing Christian cultural capital present. We are so inspired by Clement of Rome.

Christian Leaders Program of Student (September 2012)

Christian Leaders Institute is developing a ministry training program where outside textbooks are not required for ministry training. We are offering more and more classes where all digital, video and quizzing resources are in the syllabus. That means outside textbooks are not needed. Our goal is to eventually have all our courses with the resources necessary contained on the web via downloadable videos, digital context and on-line quizzes.

1. Christian Basics Certificate (7 Credits)

Students enter Christian Leaders Institute (CLI) via our Getting Started Class: Reproducible Walk with God and Christian Basics (7 credits). This class introduces students to a reproducible walk with God and grounding in historic Christian doctrine. This class gives them orientation to CLI. After they complete the Getting Started Class, students will automatically receive the Christian Basics Certificate (7 credits). This is the foundational certificate that opens up Christian Leaders Institute for further study by students.

2. Christian Leaders Certificate 23 hours)

After students complete the Christian Basics course, they are encouraged to work toward their Christian Leaders Certificate. This certificate covers the essential ministry training needed for many callings. The courses include:

- Getting Started: Reproducible Walk with God and Christian Doctrine (7 Credits)

- Old Testament Survey (3 Credits)

- New Testament Survey (3 Credits)

- Church and Ministry (3 credits)

- Pastoral Care and Marriage (3 Credits)

- Church History (4 Credits)

   Total Credits: 23

3. Commissioned Pastor Diploma (30 credit hours)

This ministry training diploma gives students the essentials they will need for leading their churches. The classes include:

- Getting Started: Reproducible Walk with God and Christian Doctrine (7 Credits)

- Church History (4 credits)

- Hermeneutics and Exegesis (3 credits)

- Preaching Methods (3 credits)

- Pastoral Care and Marriage (3 credits)

- Systematic Theology I (4 credits)

- Systematic Theology II (3 credits)

- Church and Ministry (3 credits)

   Total Credits: 30

4. Discipleship Diploma (30 credit hours)

This is the first diploma level Christian Leaders Institute offers. After a student completes the Foundational basic class, students can take any classes they want to accumulate 30 credits. This diploma is perfect for the Christian leader who wants to have a goal for continued studies. Many existing pastors may find this diploma very attractive.

- Getting Started: Reproducible Walk with God and Christian Doctrine (7 Credits)

- Christian Leaders Institute classes (23 credits)
Total Credits: 30

4. Ministry Diploma (45 Credit Hours)

The Diploma of Ministry is the first of our three advanced ministry training diplomas. This award says that students studied more areas of ministry training in-depth. This diploma will give them advanced knowledge in what they need to be a pastor, evangelist, ministry associate, church planter, chaplain, or other Christian leader. Some churches and denominations require this kind of a diploma for ordination.

- Getting Started: Reproducible Walk with God and Christian Doctrine (7 Credits)

- Old Testament Survey (3 Credits)

- New Testament Survey (3 Credits)

- Hermeneutics and Exegesis (3 credits)

- Church and Ministry (3 credits)

- Pastoral Care and Marriage (3 Credits)

- Church History (4 Credits)

- Preaching Methods (3 credits)

- Systematic Theology I (4 credits)

- Systematic Theology II (3 credits)

- Christian Ethics (3 credits)

- Christian Apologetics (3 credits)

  Required: 36 Credits
  Elective: 9 Credits
  Total 45 Credit

5. Advanced Ministry Diploma (63 credit hours)

This Advanced Diploma of Ministry gives students knowledge and insight comparable to many seminaries. More in-depth knowledge of the various areas of study will serve them well in their ministry calling. Right now, Christian Leaders Institute is developing more thought-provoking courses. CLI eventually plans to offer this diploma with an "emphasis" as our class offering increases in the next few years, Lord willing.

- Getting Started: Reproducible Walk with God and Christian Doctrine (7 Credits)

- Old Testament Survey (3 Credits)

- New Testament Survey (3 Credits)

- Hermeneutics and Exegesis (3 credits)

- Church and Ministry (3 credits)

- Pastoral Care and Marriage (3 Credits)

- Church History (4 Credits)

- Preaching Methods (3 credits)

- Systematic Theology I (4 credits)

- Systematic Theology II (3 credits)

- Christian Ethics (3 credits)

- Christian Apologetics (3 credits)

  Required: 39 Credits
  Electives: 24 Credits
  Total Credits: 63

6. Divinity Diploma (90 credit hours)

This advanced Divinity Diploma is the highest award we grant to students at Christian Leaders Institute. This diploma digs deep into every area of study for ministry training. CLI eventually plans to offer this diploma with an "emphasis" as our class offering increases in the next few years, Lord willing.

- Getting Started: Reproducible Walk with God and Christian Doctrine (7 Credits)

- Old Testament Survey (3 Credits)

- New Testament Survey (3 Credits)

- Hermeneutics and Exegesis (3 credits)

- Church and Ministry (3 credits)

- Pastoral Care and Marriage (3 Credits)

- Church History (4 Credits)

- Preaching Methods (3 credits)

- Systematic Theology I (4 credits)

- Systematic Theology II (3 credits)

- Christian Ethics (3 credits)

- Christian Apologetics (3 credits)

- Greek I (4 Credits)

- Greek II (4 Credits)

- Greek III (4 Credits)

   Required: 51 Credits
   Electives: 39 Credits
   Total: 90 Credits

Christian Leaders Institute Classes

Getting Started Class 1: Reproducible Walk with God and Christian Basics (7 Credits) Staff

This course gets you started. This course is the core orientation to Christian Leaders Institute (CLI), where you meet some of the leaders of CLI and get your computer ready for study. You will also learn a reproducible walk with God and Christian Basics. This class secures your scholarship.

After you complete this class you have full standing at Christian Leaders Institute and you receive your first certificate, the "Christian Basics Certificate. "

Old Testament Survey, Dr. David Graves and Dr. David Feddes (3 credits)

This class explores God's Word in the Old Testament, paying particular attention to literary, historical, and theological dimensions.

New Testament Survey, Rev. Pedro Aviles, Dr. Jeff Weima, and Dr. David Feddes
Supervisor: Dr. David Feddes (3 credits)

This course explores God's Word in the New Testament, paying particular attention to literary, historical, and theological dimensions.

Church History, Dr. David Feddes (4 credits)

The church is almost 2000 years old. A significant ministry training emphasis is church history. This course looks at major events and key persons in the history of the Christian church. Such study helps you to see God's faithfulness in the past and to better understand the church's present challenges and opportunities.

Pastoral Care and Marriage, Rev. Henry Reyenga Jr., Mr. Brian DeCook, Esq., Dr. Drew Brown (3 credits)

This ministry training course is essential for being an effective pastor. This course will cover listening skills, important relationship boundaries, conflict resolution, and marriage issues, including preparing couples for marriage. This important ministry training course can be taken with your spouse if you have one.

Church and Ministry, Rev. Henry Reyenga Jr. (3 credits)

This ministry training core course explores some key aspects of pastoring a church: praying, setting priorities, training other leaders, delegating, visiting, handling pressure, and more. It also offers guidance for dealing with important transitional events, such as baptisms, weddings, and funerals.

Systematic Theology I, Dr. David Feddes (4 credits)

Sound doctrine is important for ministry training. This course considers core biblical doctrines about God, humanity, Christ, the Holy Spirit, and salvation. (Can be taken either before or after Systematic Theology II).

Systematic Theology II, Dr. David Feddes (3 credits)

Ministry training must include understanding of sound doctrine. This course considers core biblical doctrines about Scripture, the church, and the future. (Can be taken either before or after Systematic Theology I).

Preaching Methods, Rev. Steve Elzinga (3 credits)

This class aims to help you "fan into flame the gift of God" (2 Tim. 1:6) in order to proclaim the Word faithfully and effectively. Areas of emphasis include: (1) blending accurate biblical interpretation with contemporary relevance; (2) preaching as an overflow of personal holiness; (3) sharpening communication skills;

and (4) integrating weekly preaching at church with daily Bible reading by the congregation at home. This is a core ministry training class that will enhance your ministry. This course also gives some basic instruction on worship issues as well.

The Craft of Preaching, Rev. Henry Reyenga (3 credits)

This class studies many of the effective preachers of the past and the present. Students will receive instruction on characteristics of preaching, watch online videos and read classic messages from featured preachers. The goal of this class is to see the craft of different preachers in order to strengthen the students voice as a preacher.

Christian Ethics, David Feddes (3 Credits)

Outside book required

This course focuses on living according to God's pattern for you. You will study biblical commands and their wise application to various life situations. You will expose demonic strategies of temptation and learn about spiritual warfare. You will seek ways to express the Christ-life within you by the power and guidance of the Holy Spirit.

Hermeneutics and Exegesis, Dr. David Feddes, Dr. Jeff Weima, and Dr. David Graves (3 credits)

How to interpret the Bible is an advanced part of your ministry training. This course deals with key issues in how to interpret the Bible. Students learn steps for studying a passage and practice using various study tools, including computer software, to become more skilled in understanding biblical passages and preparing sermons.

Christian Apologetics, Dr. Voddie Baucham and Dr. David Feddes (3 credits)

This ministry training course is designed to introduce students to basic issues in apologetics (defending and contending for the faith). The course will emphasize Biblical Worldview and Cultural Apologetics, the application of apologetics to contemporary cultural issues.

Evangelistic Missiology: Historical and Cultural Spread of Christianity, Dr. Bruce Ballast, Dr. Gary Bekker, Dr. David Feddes and Rev. Henry Reyenga (3 credits)

Once a nation or people has heard the proclamation of the gospel and the gospel is rooted and forms a culture, a spiritual warfare begins that seeks to hold back the advancement of the Kingdom of Christ. A cycle of seed sowing, cultivation, harvesting, replanting or decline, growth or revival will occur in that nation or people. This course includes some historical examination of this cycle. This class will allow you to examine the Gospel Cultivation Cycle so as to give insights on how to spread the growth of Christianity everywhere.

Biblical Greek I, Dr. David Feddes (4 credits)

This is the first in a sequence of three courses on the basics of New Testament Greek. This course takes your ministry training deeper as you study the original language the New Testament was written in.

Biblical Greek II, Dr. David Feddes (4 credits)

This is the second in a sequence of three courses on the basics of New Testament Greek. This course takes your ministry training deeper as you study the original language the New Testament was written in.

Biblical Greek III, Dr. David Feddes (4 credits)

This is the third in a sequence of three courses on the basics of New Testament Greek. If you make it this far in your Biblical Greek expertise, you will be able to read the New Testament in Greek.

Personal and Family Godliness, Rev. Joel Miller (3 credits)

An important part of your ministry training is a walk with God that is worth reproducing, and a family life that is worth multiplying.

Church Planting Action Class, Rev. Steve Elzinga, Rev. Henry Reyenga, Dr. Ron VandeGriend and Mr. Rich DeVos (9 credit)

This course helps give you the principles of church planting. This class will actually help you plant a church if that is your calling. Church planting begins with the church planted in your own life, marriage, and family. This course looks at the intentional efforts necessary to plant reproducible and sustainable churches. (Course to be ready in 2013)

Challenges in Counseling, Dr. Drew Brown (3 credits)

This course's approach to counseling blends Scripture and the soul. Starting with issues of self-discovery for the counselor himself, the course then offers a model of counseling which combines "soul care" and "spiritual direction.". Finally, we will examine how to approach some common and difficult problems in the lives of people who seek pastoral counseling: alcoholism, depression, pornography, parent-child conflict, doubt, and more.

Missiology, Dr. David Feddes (3 credit)

This ministry training course takes you into advanced missiology. This studies the culture of missions as the gospel is proclaimed through out the world

C. S Lewis and His Influence, Dr. David Feddes 3 credits

This ministry training course advances your knowledge of one of the great thinkers in Christian tradition. Get ready to be challenged.

CHAPTER 7

EVERYONE NEEDS A SPONSOR

Acts 4:36 Joseph, a Levite from Cyprus, whom the apostles called Barnabas (which means Son of Encouragement)

My family recently moved to Grand Haven, MI, USA. Our Grand Haven sponsor is Dwaine Smith, "Smitty." Smitty actually took some CLI classes. When we were thinking of moving to west Michigan, Smitty made sure that we met the pastor of their church, which also has other CLI students. He and his wife went out for coffee with my wife and me and explained many of the features of Grand Haven, Michigan. Smitty has continued to e-mail regularly about our getting settled.

He has opened up his relationship contact list and is connecting us with people we should know. His knowledge base of Grand Haven is strong, so if we have a question, he is willing to share his insights. When we need to make a decision about who are the trusted merchants, Smitty is a valuable resource. Really, Smitty is our sponsor. Without being paid or without a title, he represents the community capital of Grand Haven, and with warm hospitality, he is an open door for us to get connected both to receiving what the Grand Haven community can offer us, but also for us to contribute to building Grand Haven culture.

At Christian Leaders Institute, we see that students come to us for Biblical and academic ministry training, but we see that that ministry training is best done when a student has a sponsor or mentor. If fact, this is so important in our opinion that we ask an applying student to list their mentor/pastor/sponsor. It is this sponsor that comes on board as "adjunct faculty" with Christian Leaders Institute.

Sponsor's Call

What motivates a sponsor? A sponsor is motivated to build a culture, investing in the lives of leaders with great potential. Sponsors are motivated to help others because they love the culture they are helping to reproduce and expand.

I remember asking Rich DeVos Sr. to be my mentor/sponsor back in 1992. Rich loved the reproducing of Christianity. Based on what he learned in building Amway for a generation, he sponsored/mentored me to be introduced to ideas, people, attitudes and challenges that helped build the culture that we both loved. He freely offered recognition when I accomplished something and invested in me to bring me to even greater ministry effectiveness.

Everyone Needs to Be in a Sponsor Culture

We have invited Christian Leaders Institute students to welcome sponsors into their lives. These sponsors know the student or leader. If an existing pastor who is experienced comes into CLI for more training, we still encourage them to find a sponsor and to become one to a student. We have observed what makes an effective sponsor.

I have been a pastor since 1987, but I still need sponsors and mentors in my life. Christian Leaders Institute is entering into a new phase of existence. The founding phase is ending. Now we enter into creating an organization that will last a long time. I am going to need sponsors and mentors to teach me what I do not know and support me in what I do know.

What does a Christian Sponsor Do?

Sponsors are self-aware about their calling to build local Christian culture. In fact, they intuitively look for opportunities to help people fit in or make an impact. These sponsors know that God is calling them to invest in the lives of potential difference makers. I believe that Barnabas was a sponsor. If you look at him in relationship to Paul and Mark, you really see that his calling was to sponsor potential leaders, mentoring and making opportunities happen. Let's look at Barnabas, the father of sponsors.

I am going to list all the passages that mention the life and work of Barnabas; each of them illustrates how he was an early church sponsor. From his life, we are going to come up with a portrait of a Biblical sponsor.

1. Sponsors are Seen to Be

    Sponsors are recognized as leaders who notice those who need encouragement. Barnabas was seen that way. In fact, when he was first mentioned in the Bible by name in Acts 4:36, we see that the apostles had already changed his name from Joseph to Barnabas, which actually means Son of Encouragement:

    > Joseph, a Levite from Cyprus, whom the apostles called Barnabas (which means Son of Encouragement) (Acts 4:36)

What is interesting to note is that they gave him standing in his title. Early church titles were very important. We have the title for Jesus, "Son of God". The title for Barnabas is Son of Encouragement. A sponsor is seen to be an encourager.

If you are a student at CLI, you are encouraged to find a mentor. I encourage you to find that Barnabas who is seen to be someone who will help you. Call your mentor, "Barnabas."

If you are a mentor/sponsor, be encouraged that you fill an important role in the life of a CLI student. Be that "son of encouragement" to those who sense the calling to ministry.

2. Sponsors are Generous with Resources

Sponsors are not stingy. They take their resources of time and money and bring them to the feet of Jesus. Barnabas was generous with his resources. The second thing we read about him in the Bible is that he sold a field to help others in need:

> [Barnabas] sold a field he owned and brought the money and put it at the apostles' feet. (Acts 4:37)

Here was a guy who was already acknowledged for how he used his time to encourage others. Then on top of that he put his money where his mouth was. There was a need beyond what his encouragement brought. What did he do? Cashed in an asset to help.

This characteristic of a sponsor is so important because the new potential leader needs that model of generosity. The church needs pastors who will be willing sponsors of another generation of pastors.

3. Sponsors will make Connections

Sponsors will introduce students into opportunities. They leverage who they know to help new leaders get opportunities for ministry. Barnabas did this to the point of taking a risk. We read in Acts 9 that Saul is blinded on the road to Damascus. He is called by God to be the chosen instrument to bring the gospel to the gentiles. But Saul was known as the Christian persecutor who might be trying to play a trick on the church.

It was Barnabas who had the standing to make the introduction of Saul, later to be named Paul, to the apostles:

> When he came to Jerusalem, he tried to
> join the disciples, but they were all afraid of
> him, not believing that he really was a
> disciple. But Barnabas took him and
> brought him to the apostles. (Acts 9:26-27)

Let us be clear, a sponsor does not just connect anyone and everyone. They must have demonstrated that they are called and genuine. Barnabas saw in Saul the calling of God. It was this truth that compelled him to introduce Saul to the Apostles.

Sponsors see their role with those who God has brought to them as an opportunity to connect potential leaders with opportunities for ministry. A sponsor might help with ordination requirements at a local church or denomination. A sponsor may help connect a student with a funding opportunity.

4. Sponsors are Promoters

Sponsors speak well of those they are mentoring/sponsoring. Barnabas was one who spoke well of Saul. Barnabas saw in Saul his calling and character. I am sure he could have found a lot of negative to say about Saul. We all have that negative in us. Instead, Barnabas spoke well of the apostle and saw the positive:

> He told them how Saul on his journey had seen the Lord and that the Lord had spoken to him, and how in Damascus he had preached fearlessly in the name of Jesus. (Acts 9:27b)

Sponsors appropriately and publicly build up the potential leader. Sponsors talk that leader up. Sponsors tell positive stories about potential leaders. These potential leaders do not threaten their sponsors; their sponsors want them to succeed.

5. Sponsors Stay Connected in Ministry

Sponsors follow the ministry training progress of students and, even after they graduate, they delight in their progress and partner with them in more ministry. Barnabas was mentoring Saul when he was being prepared, he introduced him to the apostles, and even later, Barnabas went looking for Saul and then partnered in ministry with Saul for a whole year. It was at this time that the followers of Jesus were first called Christians:

> Then Barnabas went to Tarsus to look for
> Saul, and when he found him, he brought
> him to Antioch. So for a whole year
> Barnabas and Saul met with the church and
> taught great numbers of people. The
> disciples were called Christians first at
> Antioch. (Acts 11:25-26)

Ministry capital is ultimately about leaders partnering together and building a culture that honors Christ. Those who go before students, later work with those very students. Sponsors really stay connected with their potential leaders even after they have left the preparation stage and are now ministering. Saul and Barnabas made such a team that the apostles sent them on a mission together:

> While they were worshiping the Lord and
> fasting, the Holy Spirit said, "Set apart for
> me Barnabas and Saul for the work to which
> I have called them." (Acts 13:2)

6. Sponsors Who become Less

There will be times when the one in training will be called to a special work by God. The sponsored one will succeed beyond his sponsor and mentor. Saul's name is changed to Paul and he is now the team leader. In Chapter 13 of Acts, Barnabas is still mentioned first, "the Holy Spirit said, "Set apart for me Barnabas and Saul for the work to which I have called them." But now Chapter 14 mentions Paul first:

> Paul and Barnabas appointed elders for them in each church and, with prayer and fasting, committed them to the Lord, in whom they had put their trust. (Acts 14:23)

An effective sponsor/mentor is looking for people who will exceed them in impact. They will invest and encourage leaders to be their best for God. Paul and Barnabas were together planting churches and appointing leaders everywhere they went.

7. Sponsor and Sponsored not Afraid of Doing Their Own Thing

The relationship of the sponsor and the sponsored can change even as circumstances change. Paul and Barnabas parted company over a disagreement. I am so glad this stayed in the Bible. Sometimes a sponsor and the one who is sponsored disagree about something. Barnabas and Paul so disagreed about what to do with Mark that they parted company.

Barnabas appeared to want to give Mark another opportunity to prove himself in ministry. Paul felt that it was risky to take someone who had buckled under pressure. When reading about their disagreement, I am impressed that they both went their own way and God's kingdom was advanced in their disagreement:

> Some time later Paul said to Barnabas, "Let us go back and visit the brothers in all the towns where we preached the word of the Lord and see how they are doing." Barnabas wanted to take John, also called Mark, with them, but Paul did not think it wise to take him, because he had deserted them in Pamphylia and had not continued with them in the work. They had such a sharp disagreement that they parted company. Barnabas took Mark and sailed for Cyprus. but Paul chose Silas and left, commended by the brothers to the grace of the Lord. (Acts 15:36-40)

Sometimes the sponsor and the sponsored have disagreements, even sharp ones. I have seen a sponsored student sense the call to plant a new church. The sponsor disagrees. Eventually the sponsor and the sponsored part company. At first they are uncomfortable about the split, but eventually they not only talk to each other, but the kingdom of God is advanced as well.

At Christian Leaders Institute, sponsors and mentors are such an asset for the student. When sponsors give students opportunities to preach, lead and pray, the student greatly benefits.

More and more, Christian Leaders Institute will connect and build the connection between sponsor and the sponsored. Christian Leaders Institute will deliver high-quality Biblical ministry training, and sponsors will do the finishing touches and provide a local context to the students. This will keep students' blooming where they are planted.

Sponsors Connect Students with Ministry Capital

Adoniram Judson had little, if any, cultural capital to work with as he proclaimed the gospel in Burma. In most countries and urban areas there is, in modern times, at least some, and sometimes a lot, of Christianity social capital. Christian Leaders Institute wants to focus on imparting some tried and true ministry training resources, understanding that we will only be a part of the picture in building Christian culture.

Sponsors will connect students in a culture so that they will be able to more effectively minister in that culture. Sponsors will play an important role in connecting students to the people, expectations, and opportunities for effective ministry. When we have a system of ministry training that does not keep the person connected, we will often limit that leader's impact. Social capital is very important. It always has been, if a student misses out on this connecting, that student has to create his/her own social capital from scratch.

Ministry Training Expectations and Social Capital

I believe we should talk a little about social capital of Christian culture and ministry training expectations.

The elements of building a Christian capital must include a self-aware discussion of what makes a Christian culture sustainable for generations. I also find the topic of ministry training fascinating in relationship to how that training functions within a specific people group. Each people group has different expectations for ministry training steps, which are very connected to the Christian vitality that is at their disposal. New groups will create new expectations.

I am Dutch by ethnic background, and ordained in the
Christian Reformed Church (CRC) in North America.
When called into the ministry, I benefited from an entire
Christian social capital that supported me in receiving
the training I needed. The ministry training place that
was selected to train ministers was Calvin Theological
Seminary. I attended there for four years and loved
every moment of that experience.

After my calling to the ministry, my local church prayed
for, gave endorsement to and supported my ministry
calling. The local group of churches, which was called a
Classis, actually had a student fund committee to help
pay for tuition both at my college and seminary level.
When I went to Calvin Seminary, the Christian Reformed
denomination "taxed" every church and encouraged
every church to give a "ministry share" that supported
Calvin to keep tuition down for those from the Christian
Reformed Church.

Since there were lots of Christian Reformed Churches
near the seminary, and many businesses that had a soft
spot for future Christian Reformed leaders, my wife and
I both easily found jobs at businesses and churches. I did
not need to assume much debt for my ministry training,
since Pam and I worked. Even if I did assume debt, I was
reasonably assured that there was a church out there
who would "call" me to be their pastor. Christian

Reformed pastors generally have been fairly well compensated, so that whatever debts they did incur could be repaid in due time.

In addition to this, the Christian Reformed church experienced, in those days, a great homogeneity. Most of us were Dutch Christians. This contributed to clearer communication and common experience with certain themes agreed upon. Immigrant Christian Dutch people in my childhood were very hard-working, moderate people who prized academics, cleanliness, daily Bible reading and prayer, Sunday observance and doctrinal training.

In addition to this, the Christian Reformed Church was very supportive of a Christian School movement that functioned in many places as a 5 day a week "program of the denomination." In addition to this, the Dutch people were a wealthy group, second only behind Jewish Americans in this wealth.

New Ministry Training Expectations developed in the Christian Reformed Church as new peoples were reached through the mission efforts of Home Missions, the local mission support organization of the denomination.

In the early nineteen-nineties, alternate routes to the ministry were being emphasized. These routes were always technically allowed, but not really pursued by many called leaders. There was much resistance by many in the people group to alternate routes to ministry.

It was as if CRC ministry candidates needed to be prepared in a way that took in all the pillars of Christian Reformed homogeneous Dutch culture. Those who entered the CRC in a different way many times did not feel that they were "real" ministers of the Word. By 2002, they were actually named Ministry Associates. By 2008, these ministry associates were allowed to do everything a minister of the Word could do, as long as the group of Ministers of the Word and Elders in a given region, named the Classis, gave permission for them to minister in a local context with a local job description.

Two main ministry cultivation paths were now side by side: The path for ministry associate and the path for ministry of the Word. The ministry associate path was more grass-roots, and the academic training included what the local mentoring group thought was important. In 2012, the name ministry associate was changed to Commissioned Pastor to indicate that these leaders are not second-rate ministry leaders.

The Minister of the Word training include an accredited academic training and leaders were encouraged to go to Calvin Seminary. If they went to another seminary, they still had some requirements for Calvin Seminary training, which is still true today.

Christian Leaders Institute has increasingly been training Commissioned pastors to give them an excellent academic ministry training that is Biblical, Theological, and practical. This ministry training is closing the gap between those who are trained at Calvin Seminary and those who are not.

Calvin Seminary fills the central role for the majority of expectations for ministry training preparation for a large segment of the Christian Reformed Church. As the Christian Reformed church grows, Christian Leaders Institute may help many in this denomination to get excellent ministry training in new co-people groups that arise within the Christian Reformed Church.

In every denomination, these dynamics, though different within each people group, function to create expectations for ministry training. These expectations take centuries to form, and they include many social, economic, and cultural factors. These expectations adjust as people groups change or new ones are formed.

Christian Leaders Institute is leveraging capital from what we have been given and bringing the capital in the service of training as many people as possible who are called into ministry. Christian Leaders Institute is not affiliated with any denomination, we minister now to a large segment of the evangelical world, but are thankful for ministry capital we received as we offer training free of charge to any called leader.

Sponsors Bring Ministry Opportunities

The sponsors in a local people group really are important. These sponsors will help students interface with their group. These sponsors will make sure that there is a path of ordination for the student when they complete their training. The sponsors will help students plug in and help them in their ordination at a local church or in a church planting situation. CLI can bring excellent ministry training to the students; the sponsor can bring excellent ministry opportunity to the students.

As Christian Leaders Institute grows, we will also grow in our desire to connect each student in their area with sponsors who will help them connect to the ministry capital that God has been creating for centuries.

CHAPTER 8

EVERYONE IS A SPONSOR

<u>1 Thessalonians 5:11</u> Therefore encourage one another and build each other up, just as in fact you are doing.

I remember in 1994 when Rich DeVos began to mentor me. I decided to join Amway as a business owner associate. I decided to join because I reasoned that if the co-founder of Amway was mentoring me, I should walk the path he helped create. My Amway experience was excellent.

I saw ordinary men and women do extraordinary things. People, that you would not think could build a business, actually succeeded. I also saw that people, who looked like they had the complete package to build a business, quit after a couple of weeks. I signed up over 80 new distributors in 6 months and really enjoyed the business. In fact, I had to figure out whether being an Amway distributor was my calling. After careful prayer and reflection, I renewed my resolve for ministry.

I learned much as an Amway distributor, by the way I saw all these values up close and personal in Rich DeVos. He modeled and understood being a leader. I learned about so much that goes into building anything including a business, a church, and even an online Bible school. These things have helped me greatly in life and have laid the foundation for so much of what I have been called to pursue. I learned things like:

1. Getting over the fear of meeting and talking to people, letting respect and love guide me.

   Treat everyone as an image bearer of God who is worth my time in that moment. People will see an elitist heart; they will sense if I only talk to them if I have a hidden agenda. I learned that God has a plan in every relationship He puts in my life.

2. Be a servant leader, not just an authority leader.

3. Leaders create stages for others to do well.

   Jesus himself said to his disciples, "Anyone who wants to be first must be the very last, and the servant of all." (Mark 9:35). People sense if I have their best interest in mind or mine.

4. Work hard in a focused way.

   Hard work is a given. Focused hard work makes the most difference. For instance, sitting at the computer conducting research about selling is not actually selling.

5. Recruit everyone, but when you find leaders, train them well.

   Leaders are the key to building anything sustainable. If you want to build a movement, look for leaders and give them the training they need to succeed.

6. Create a culture of reproducible knowledge, habits and sharing.

   If I wanted to build an Amway business, those I sponsored needed some knowledge of the products and the Amway way. They needed to use the products habitually, and they needed to learn how to share what they used in their personal life. I sponsored an Egyptian neighbor who snuck in our kitchen while at our house and checked our cupboards to see if my wife and I used Amway products.

This is so similar in Christianity. Christians get saved into a walk with God. They need knowledge of what Christianity actually is about. Someone needs to teach them who the God of the Bible is and how to walk with him. Someone needs to be able to communicate basic Bible teaching. Knowledge is very important.

Then there is the need to walk in daily habits. This walk with God is simple, involving talking and listening daily in their personal life, their marriage (if married), their family, their friends, their church and their connection to other Christians worldwide. They need to walk in a path of sharing their walk with God. This simple walk with God in Christ has been reproducible for 2000 years.

7. Recognize Achievements.

When someone does well, say so. Be real about this, but do not err on the stingy side of encouragement. I saw how important recognition was while doing an Amway business. This recognition would bring people to tears because they never thought someone noticed what they did.

Many times, Christians do not encourage or compliment those who are faithful in building up the church, because we do not want pride to characterize our churches. But the Bible does teach that we ought to recognize those who live according to the pattern that was given. Philippians 3:17 says, "Join with others in following my example, brothers, and take note of those who live according to the pattern we gave you."

8. See the potential in people without prequalifying them.

Rich DeVos sure practiced what he preached. From day one in our mentoring relationship, Rich saw the potential in me despite the fact that I had and still have such a long way to go. The Amway organization teaches this as a core value. So many of their leaders are now leaders because someone gave them an opportunity to start a business at almost no start-up capital. Successful Amway associates were a delight to be around because they were often intrinsically motivated to do the business out of passion and calling and not out of the force of debt.

At Christian Leaders Institute, we are trying to allow leaders and potential leaders to get their ministry training to become a pastor at little cost, so that everyone who is called gets an opportunity. This is such a core value that we have learned to keep operating expenses so low that everyone who finishes the getting started class gets free tuition.

We do ask students to donate to help other students get the training. We find that the students that finish the getting started class are intrinsically motivated to do their studies. A large investment of money or relocation is not the force that motivates them to complete their studies. They complete their training because they know they need it. Plus, the low cost to each student allows students from the poorest of poor countries and students from anywhere to get training no matter what their situation is like.

9. Use technology to serve your purpose.

   I always loved this about Amway. In the early 1990s, when I was involved with Amway, they were always at the cutting edge of using technology to help their leaders do better. Today, I understand that so much of the business is driven by effective use of the internet.

   As we talked about earlier in this book, the conversion box of the internet was invented and this is a powerful tool now spreading to bring high quality ministry training everywhere.

10. Build where you are and with the people you are with.

   Rich would encourage me to help people bloom where they were planted. The Amway leaders would help each person write down on a piece of paper everyone they knew, so that they could contact each of them to promote their products. Some people did not like this, but this is really where the leaders are discovered. If leaders will share their passion and products with those they know, they will be more likely to share their passion and their products with people they do not know.

Christian Leaders Institute is all about having leaders bloom where they are planted. We bring the training to students' homes, to their context with their sponsors. We believe that there already exists relational capital that can be built on for the gospel of Jesus Christ and the building and the strengthening of the Church.

I am so happy and feel so blessed by the mentorship and sponsorship from Rich DeVos, one of the founding board members of Christian Leaders Institute. As I look at what Amway has done from thirty-thousand feet it is very much similar to the topic of this book. Amway was about planting a culture of entrepreneurship, a culture where anyone can be a business owner.

This culture is not just about selling books and tapes about how to build businesses; this is a culture where there are actually products and services used by real people. This culture builds to where now Amway is world-wide and there are products and services available everywhere, but more importantly, there are business owners who are leaders in their cultures. The leaders bloom where they are planted and they start reaching people who reach even more people. This culture keeps spreading and includes more and more leaders everyday.

At the thirty-thousand foot view level, I noticed that every successful Amway distributor was a product user themselves and that now they too were sponsoring others like they were sponsored. This meant that they committed to a product-use lifestyle and they trained, and boldly sponsored, others into that lifestyle. Some of the most fearless people I have ever seen were Amway business owners. I always admired that boldness. I also noticed that these distributors got into the habit of helping people even when it had nothing to do with Amway. They sponsored people into a better life, whatever that would mean in that local context.

Everyone is A Sponsor

My involvement with Amway illustrated something that was just plain true. Sponsors make a culture grow. And whether a formal system like Amway, where every relationship is kept track of, or in informal relationships, leaders step forward to create culture. Sponsors make things happen. Sponsors really are the leaders of a society. I have noticed that most people have a few topics where they would be considered "sponsors." Just get someone talking about what interests them and you will find that they willingly lead others in their pursuits. It appears that everyone is building something metaphorically. I got so interested in having Rich DeVos mentor me in 1994 because I had seen an enthusiastic Amway distributor attempt to get me to join Amway, and he impressed me.

I concluded that we needed that kind of enthusiasm in Christians sponsoring their neighbors into a walk with God. I realize that we do not want to be annoying or too pushy, but who can fault us for our passion, love and concern for our fellow humans. If Christianity is true, and we believe it to be, we can't just sit back and say "whatever." We really need to participate in sponsoring this eternal salvation culture to spread through the entire earth.

So while we enjoy many passions and activities on this earth, we need to realize that each of us also is a sponsor in building Christianity. In Christianity, we can take on different types of sponsoring roles, but we are still nonetheless called to build with our time, talents and resources.

Become Sponsors at Christian Leaders Institute

There are many ways to sponsor the building of leader culture at Christian Leaders Institute. But to me, it is like what Amway does in the area of business ownership.

Amway wins when people with the dream to build a business get that opportunity. Business owners are not working for Amway; they are working on building on their dreams to build their business. They can take those dreams as far as they want to go. Both on the ministry side, the encouragement side and the fundraising money to support CLI side, we have the same attitude.

Ministry Opportunities

On the ministry side, we give students in whatever their situation the opportunity to go as far as they want to go. In the year 2012-2013 this means that 14,000 new applications were taken and these students were given an account to be a student at Christian Leaders Institute. They were given their "kit," called the Getting Started Class; that kit was free. All they had to invest was their time and an Internet connection. Of those 14,000 new students, over 1,200 of them completed the Getting Started Class and went deeper into their ministry training. These students were plugged in with their local mentor/sponsor. A growing number of students from all over the world are now even donating money to sponsor others in gaining quality ministry training.

Encouragement Opportunities

On the encouragement side, we started an encouragement program for Christians who wanted to become, like Barnabas, a son or daughter of encouragement. We give mature believers an opportunity to bring a mission trip right into their homes or businesses. If your calling is to connect, pray and encourage ministry students to finish their preparations, we want to partner with you and give you the encouragement "kit" to prepare you to be an encourager at CLI.

This encouragement program is for pastors, former students, mature Christians, and donors to Christian Leaders Institute. This program takes encouragers on a "Barnabas trip." Encouragers take a "getting started class" and are taught how to directly talk to current students and encourage them in their calling.

If you are reading this book and desire to encourage our students, go to www.christianleader.net to find out more information.

Donation Opportunities

On the donation side, we are giving opportunities for sponsors to make an investment in the preparation of called Christian leaders. We have profiles ready to give donors tangible evidence that their support of CLI is really leveraging their calling to utilize their resources effectively, and as a steward of their resources, build the kingdom of God.

We respect the fact that every Christian donor has a calling to build the kingdom of God. Our goal is to serve their dream. It is not so much that they support us, now we support them in their calling to give and make an impact. When donors give gifts to CLI, we think of it as directly and efficiently sponsoring ministry globally. We want to help Christians sponsor as much building of Christian ministry capital as possible.

Reasons to Financially Sponsor Leaders for Ministry Training

As you pray and think about where you will invest your resources, I ask that you will consider these reasons for sponsoring ministry leaders at Christian Leaders Institute.

1. Build on the missions movement of the past, training the children of that movement. The Internet is increasingly available even in the remotest parts of the world. Christian Leaders Institute will bring your sponsorship there.

2. Efficiently invest your mission capital to make a large impact. Christian Leaders Institute is very efficient in leveraging your resources. A typical seminary needs from $10,000 to $40,000 per

student per year to deliver high-quality ministry training. Christian Leaders Institute has got this training cost down to $600 dollars per year per student.

Courses are designed to be completely web Indigenous, updated, improved, used again and again. We put up courses from academically trained and ministry tested professors who hold higher degrees from accredited institutions. We video these professors and use their course materials again and again.

Our content can come from previously recorded video content, including deceased leaders like Dr. Francis Schaeffer or retired leaders like Dr. Ed Roels, and in partnership with organizations like Vision Video.

Our fundraising ratios have historically been very low with administration and fundraising below 5 percent of the budget. We plan to keep this as low as possible. We are hoping to keep that percentage below 20 percent of the budget.

Jennifer Santo wanted us to let her thank you for what this training means to her.

"Hello generous donors. I am greatly appreciative of those of you that donate to Christian Leaders Institute. With this help, I will be able to achieve the goals Christ has set out for my life. I want to help those outside that have felt like they have no hope to live for. My father used to be a severe drug addict and alcoholic. I grew up in that environment believing that was normal, but when I gave my life to Christ I realized there was an even deeper issue. My dad needed God's love more than ever because he was headed down a life of total ruin.

I want to help people like my dad. I want those types of people to be able to have a second chance at life, to be able to know that there are more reasons to live than to die. I've always wanted to go to a Bible institute, but could not afford it. With this opportunity to have a free scholarship, it means the world to me to be able to enhance my knowledge of God's perfect word. God is good. I came to Christ in October 2006. That was when I met the love of my life, my boyfriend. He has helped me so much and he was the one that took me to his church where I am now a member.

I am not involved in ministry right now, but that is why I joined Christian Leaders Institute. I feel God's calling on my life right now, and I am responding to this calling. I pray God expands my wisdom of His word and continues to show me to believe in Him and believe in myself. I do not want to underestimate myself, but I want to believe that the power invested in me has been given to me by God. Just as he did for Moses, Paul, and even Jesus, God can do for me."

3. Get involved as an encourager. You are invited to become an encourager. Being an encourager is like taking a missions trip in other organizations. Missions trips can be expensive, and though

important in the work of raising money in these organizations, we can bring a missions trip to you. If you go to www.christianleaders.net, you can sign up to be an encourager. You will talk with and pray for students as they pursue their ministry training. You will be encouraged as you are encouraging.

4. Become a student. Many supporters of Christian Leaders Institute have become students themselves. Just sign up as a student and take some classes. Sponsor the opportunity and enjoy that opportunity for yourself, your spouse, your children and your church. Refer this opportunity to anyone you know. Last year, my twelve-year-old daughter took Greek online at CLI. We make this ministry available to you or any one you know.

5. Become a sponsor of other sponsors. You can leverage your gifts to build the Kingdom of God via CLI. If you will sponsor, that is, lead other sponsors, who hopefully will lead other sponsors to sponsor the building of ministry training, we could reach thousands more leaders. This would mean impact for thousands or even millions of lives. Christian Leaders Institute is very scalable. We believe that we can reach more people as more resources are invested.

Hear the call to build the kingdom, with Christian Leaders Institute helping you make a bigger impact.

Train at Christian Leaders

If you are sensing the call into ministry, CLI will give you the opportunity to explore that calling and receive training free of charge.
www.christianleadersinstitute.org

If you are feeling called to pray and encourage, join the encourager program at www.christianleaders.net

If you are wondering where to invest to make the most possible impact with your missions dollars, we would like the privilege to serve you. If you are a foundation and you want to continue to leverage your impact in missions, please consider Christian Leaders Institute. If you want to sponsor a student at $600 dollars for a year of study or just make an investment of any amount go to www.openthedoorwide.org

Let's build and strengthen the church together, as students, encouragers and donors, so that the gospel continues to reach and transform this world.

2 Corinthians 4:15 "All this is for your benefit, so that the grace that is reaching more and more people may cause thanksgiving to overflow to the glory of God."

CHRISTIAN LEADERS INSTITUTE

Donor Information (please print) or visit
www.christianleaders.net/donate

Name _____

Address _____

City, ST Zip
Code _____

Phone: _____

Email _____

I (we) pledge a total of $_____ to be paid: ☐now
☐monthly ☐quarterly ☐yearly.

I (we) plan to make this contribution in the form of: ☐cash ☐check
☐credit card ☐other. In the USA, we will send you a receipt for your
tax deductible donation

Credit card type |
Exp. date _____

Credit card number _____

Authorized signature _____

☐form enclosed ☐form will be forwarded

Please make checks, or other gifts
payable to:

Christian Leaders Institute
14367 West 159th Street
Homer Glen, IL 60491

CHRISTIAN
LEADERS
INSTITUTE   Tear This Form Out

Donor Information (please print) or visit
www.christianleaders.net/donate

Name _____

Address _____

City, ST Zip
Code _____

Phone: _____

Email _____

I (we) pledge a total of $_____ to be paid: ▢now
▢monthly ▢quarterly ▢yearly.

I (we) plan to make this contribution in the form of: ▢cash ▢check
▢credit card ▢other. In the USA, we will send you a receipt for your
tax deductible donation.

Credit card type |
Exp. date _____

Credit card number _____

Authorized signature _____

▢form enclosed ▢form will be forwarded

Please make checks, or other gifts | Christian Leaders Institute
payable to: | 14367 West 159th Street
| Homer Glen, IL 60491

CHRISTIAN LEADERS INSTITUTE Tear This Form Out

Donor Information (please print) or visit
www.christianleaders.net/donate

Name _____

Address _____

City, ST Zip
Code _____

Phone: _____

Email _____

I (we) pledge a total of $_____ to be paid: ⬜now
⬜monthly ⬜quarterly ⬜yearly.

I (we) plan to make this contribution in the form of: ⬜cash ⬜check
⬜credit card ⬜other. In the USA, we will send you a receipt for your
tax deductible donation.

Credit card type |
Exp. date _____

Credit card number _____

Authorized signature _____

⬜form enclosed ⬜form will be forwarded

Please make checks, or other gifts payable to:
Christian Leaders Institute
14367 West 159th Street
Homer Glen, IL 60491

ABOUT THE AUTHOR

Henry Reyenga Jr. has planted four new churches and has replanted one in the United States of America. He has worked for the international ministry of the Bible League for four years. He has been a pastor since 1988. In 2002, Henry founded Christian Leaders Institute which started offering Internet classes in 2006. In 2012, over 14,000 new students enrolled at Christian Leaders Institute.

Henry Reyenga is married to Pam Reyenga, they five children and eight grandchildren.

Made in the USA
Charleston, SC
14 November 2012